"Mary MacRory's wonderful book will help you to identify your goals, get properly motivated and show you how to take action and achieve your big dreams!"

Victoria Mary Clarke, Media Coach, Art of Living Radio and Author

"Mary MacRory is clearly a woman wanting to help other women flourish in life. She covers many topics offering a broad spectrum of self-help tools, different perspectives and ideas to choose from. This is a book that both informs and enables. "

Dr. Lynda Shaw, Neuroscientist, Business Psychologist, Speaker, Author

"As someone who swears by the morning journal, I believe 'Women. Work and Wellness' is a must read to help you understand various techniques which you can then incorporate into your life. I particularly like the exercises that are included throughout the book."

Patricia Gibney, International Best-selling Author

WOMEN, WORK AND WELLNESS

Mary MacRory

New Generation Publishing

Are you an employee, self-employed, a business owner, or someone wishing to start your own business? Are you considering a complete lifestyle change?

If yes – then this book is for you. It is a practical, up-to-date guide for everyone, especially working women, so that you can make that transformational journey and arrive at your destination experiencing more understanding of yourself, feeling more empowered and with more enjoyment and fulfilment in both your personal and work life.

This book will help you to understand more about:

- Your inner self, how your mind and body work so that you can optimise the way that you think and feel.

- The process to enable you to move forward from your dreams to make step-by-step plans to achieve the life, career or business goals you genuinely want.

- The link between the Law of Attraction, your energy levels, manifestation and achieving success. How your energy levels, needs, thoughts, behaviours and the chakras are connected. Some helpful tools and techniques to maximise a positive outcome for you.

- Shifting negative behaviours - procrastination, fear of stepping out of your comfort zone, overwhelm, self-sabotage. Practical and effective Time Management strategies.

- Self-care and tools, tips and techniques for maintaining positive, high energy. Understanding and using the power of gratitude, effective visualisation and affirmations. Exploring techniques of anchoring, meditation, Neuro Linguistic Programming (NLP) and Quantum Thinking Technologies (QTT).

- Being aware of the nature of coaching and other holistic therapies and how they can help you to have a less stressed, more balanced, enjoyable and successful lifestyle.

- Practical advice on making career strides in the Corporate Sector tailored especially for women and relevant to Human Resources (HR) Professionals.

- Available resources to help you on your journey, examining mainstream and holistic therapies.

Everyone can learn from this book, as it is just as applicable to men as it is to women, despite the title! I have included some of my own life experiences and learnings in the book as I passionately believe that we should be working and living well as that is what we deserve. I have been very honest in this as I want to authentically enable people to live better lives. So, it is a self-help book with several autobiographical insights included.

There are also wellness ideas to re-energise stressed workforces that HR professionals may be interested in. Staff morale and wellness are so important for everyone and are essential considerations in running productive and ethically aware businesses. That is another important reason why I have written this book. Enjoy!

Mary MacRory

B Sc. (Joint Hons), Durham University, UK.

Fellow of Association of Chartered Certified Accountants (FCCA).

SNHS Dip. Life Coaching – with Distinction and Accredited by and a member of the International College of Holistic Medicine (ICHM).

Certified as Practitioner in Neuro-Linguistic Programming (NLP).

Certified as Quantum Thinking Technologist (QTT).
Quantum Release.
Quantum Alignment.
Seven Behavioural Codes (Mind Experts Academy).

Alternative Dispute Resolution (ACCA CPD Course).

Certificate with Distinction in Training and Continuing Development (NUI Maynooth).

Reiki Master in the lineage of Usui-Hayashi-Takata-Twan-Claff/O'Reilly-Ryan

Acknowledgements

To everybody who has helped me and whom I have helped and learned from – a big thank you. There are too many people to individually name who have contributed positively to my life but the Donlon family from County Longford in Ireland (my mother was a Donlon) are right up there! I also want to thank all my school (Middlesbrough) and university friends (Durham) strewn all over England, Ireland and Australia who still are true gems. Thanks to the amazing (and less amazing) work colleagues at every level who have provided me with invaluable insights.

Special mention to Cissi Kansky, Moira Geary, Victoria Mary Clarke, Vanessa O'Loughlin-Fox, Susan Yeates, Orla O'Rourke, Trudy Ryan, Carolin Soldo, Belinda Ginter, Alison Martin, Mary Donlon, Patricia Gibney and Breda Stackpool, all of whom have given me wise and practical advice.

Thank you to all my friends everywhere and to the hugely inspiring and supportive coaches and Quantum Thinking practitioners that I have had the pleasure to meet and work with throughout my own training and practice.

Last, but certainly not least, to my husband, Dan and to Colleen and Shane, my two adult children. I am proud of you all and of what we have learned from each other and achieved so far on our journey through life.

marymacrory

TABLE OF CONTENTS

INTRODUCTION

I am writing this book to provide a comprehensive, practical, helpful and up-to-date guide for everyone, but particularly for working women, who juggle their careers and family lives often under enormous stress. It is based upon my own experience, working up to a senior level in Finance, running successful businesses, raising two children with ageing parents and looking to enjoy my life, as indeed, we all strive to do. I decided to take a completely different focus so took a step back and embarked upon a Personal Development Course (Wealthy Minds), studied Neuro Linguistic Programming (NLP) and Quantitative Thinking Technologies (QTT - developed by Moira Geary) and I am continuing my journey learning from various therapies – both holistic and mainstream. I had originally decided to do this work purely for myself. However, I quickly realised that I could help other people and that is one of the main reasons that I went on to study for a Life Coaching Diploma and was also the main inspiration for my writing this book.

I made my own transformational journey by leaving behind the low-energy, stressed, stuck and not particularly joyful state I was in. I wanted to progress to vibrate at a higher energy level, feel more empowered and achieve a happier and more peaceful state of mind. It has been quite a learning experience. It can also serve as a very useful map for anyone else who is in a similar situation and is looking to make that transformational journey for themselves.

What does all this mean for you?

- I am providing practical advice, tips and techniques if you are that person who has lost focus on what is genuinely important to you in your life. I help you to get back on track or maybe even to change lifestyle or career direction, if that is what turns out to be what serves you the best.

- Enabling you to shift negative mindsets and blocks that are holding you back. Allowing you to then flourish and prosper in a positive and a more joyful and peaceful state.

- Helping you to deal more effectively with managing your time so that you do not become overwhelmed. By effectively managing your time and dealing with overwhelm, you will not be frozen and stuck like a rabbit in the headlights. You will be able to confidently deal with the myriad of tasks that life and work throw at you. You will enjoy the challenges, become empowered and strengthened by your successes.

- Providing you with practical strategies to manage your stress levels. You can regain control of your life, address the "burnt-out" feeling and instead, relish and confidently embrace the challenges you face daily. It is a great feeling to regain perspective and control of your life.

- Offering you practical strategies for self-care that will build you up so that you are not constantly stressed but instead relish challenges and positively look forward to actioning your plans and achieving those goals. All done with the intention of improving some or all aspects of your life and lifestyle, rather than approaching life from a fearful perspective.

- Suggesting advice that is very much based upon my own corporate experience regarding progressing through the ranks and enjoying the corporate game, if that is your chosen path. This can of course change should you desire to step out of this culture and lifestyle and that is all good too. I have added in some summary advice regarding setting up your own business as I have considerable practical experience in this area both as a professional accountant and as a coach.

- Explaining the nature and uses of various mainstream and holistic therapies and how they can fit into your sustainable self-care regime so that you feel more relaxed, receive improved health benefits and experience a greater joy and peace in your life.

All these scenarios above represent situations that I was striving to come to terms with, within my own life. My intention being to recapture the enjoyment I once had in my younger days. By finding solutions to resolve these situations, I decided to not only adopt a new and better lifestyle but also to share the learnings so that everyone can benefit.

There is absolutely no need for anyone to be suffering silently in pain when there are solutions available to release on that pain and to allow personal growth in its place.

How to get the best use out of this book

Everyone is busy with many demands on their time, consequently, I have deliberately written this book in a very structured way so that you can easily dip into the chapters (or sections within the chapters) that interest you the most. You can select, the specific topics where you feel you will gain some useful tips or information.

The Journey itself is basically charted in the various chapters. These are arranged in a logical sequence starting from where you are now – your current state – to the desired or final state where you want to be.

A summary of the journey in this book is shown below:

CURRENT STATE

Low energy
Over-stressed
Lack of enjoyment
Personally stuck
Professionally stuck

JOURNEY

Tools, tips and techniques from:
Life Coaching
NLP
QTT
Life and business experience
Modern research
Established learnings
Holistic techniques

FINAL STATE

High energy
Healthy stress levels
Empowered, confident and happy
Personally flourishing
Professionally flourishing

ABOUT THE AUTHOR

Initially, gaining a Joint Honours Science degree (Botany and Physical Geography) at Durham University in the UK, I had intended to study and pursue a career in Landscape Architecture. However, with the economic turmoil in the UK in 1978 and having earlier experienced the 3-day week, I decided to relocate to Ireland, my spiritual home and pursue another career. A pragmatic decision to earn money, rather than for any other reason, determined my choice to train in Dublin as an accountant. This is the field I have since worked in for thirty-eight years, until I made a conscious career change to leave the corporate world and become a Life and Business Coach.

When I was a single person with no children, life was relatively stress-free. However, when children and family life came into play, I found that the stress levels from all directions increased. I have had a successful career within Accountancy but in common with many working in this and in several other fields, the long hours can be quite a strain after many years. This stress increases when adding in growing families and ageing parents.

Within my own working life, I have noticed that many women, myself included, often put themselves last after family and work demands. This can eventually result in a lack of joy and sometimes a general dissatisfaction in our lives due to stress levels not being managed properly. Time being at a premium, there is also not a lot of spare time to devote to our own relaxation. This may not be fully appreciated by us or by others, especially in what is still basically a patriarchal corporate world and society. Things are changing but this book is specifically written to give useful tips and techniques that I would have loved to have known when going through some of the most stressful and painful times in my own life. It would have made me take more time for my own self-care and generally to feel less guilt and anxiety.

As my awareness of the practical challenges grew and with the children now adults, I decided to leave the corporate Accountancy world and to research what exactly could be done to improve life and work satisfaction for myself and for working women. Initially, this was purely for my own reasons but as stated, I soon realised that this knowledge and the benefits gleaned, could and should be shared with other women (and men) still in that situation. I have always been interested in psychology, mentoring and in coaching both inside and outside of my work. Together with having practical as well as theoretical experience in coaching, mentoring, NLP and QTT, I realised that now was the time to embrace the challenge and share this knowledge and experience both within my coaching career and in this book.

The phrase "work-life balance", whilst often quoted on company websites and when staff are being recruited, is generally not put into practice within the working environment. So, in this book, I have drawn upon my own considerable experiences, plus those of others, various pieces of new research and articles in addition to several certified courses to pull together a much needed, up-to-date guide on practical ways to assist women (and men) to live more empowered, satisfying personal and professional lives.

I hope it helps you to understand and more successfully navigate work and life with more effectiveness, efficiency and enjoyment. So much is known today about how our subconscious mind works and how we can optimise our behavioural patterns, manage our time and stress better and basically, enjoy all aspects of our life more. The knowledge needs to be shared and I believe some aspects should even be taught in schools. It is very heartening to see that an increasing number of UK and Irish schools are introducing mindfulness classes to children as young as six and seven. It is great to instil positive, calming habits into young minds so that they can draw on this inner strength in years to come.

My offering to you in this book – is to provide a useful and practical guide to living happier, more stress-free personal and professional lives, whether working as a paid employee, owning your own business or wanting to make a lifestyle change (that may even include starting up your own business).

If you enjoyed this book and would like to work with me further or share with me how the book has changed your work-life satisfaction, please visit my website www.marymacrory.com, my Facebook page or on LinkedIn and Instagram, where we can stay in touch.

Chapter 1

The Need for Self-Knowledge

Role of the Subconscious Mind

We make approximately 90% of our decisions using the subconscious part of our brain. This makes perfect sense as normal bodily functions such as breathing or digestion do not require us to take a logical, conscious decision each time every one of these activities occur.

Whilst this is a very good and practical arrangement, as we go from birth – where literally, our subconscious mind is a blank canvas – through life, we also absorb many experiences which are stored in the subconscious. In addition, the subconscious stores meanings and feelings associated with these stored memories. Over time the memories, complete with the associated feelings, can become embedded in positive (or negative) behavioural patterns and beliefs. We may not even be aware that we possess some of these feelings, beliefs and associated memories.

The primary function of the subconscious is to protect us and it does this in two ways:

1. Physically: it controls breathing, blinking, digestion, responses to danger for example.

2. Emotionally: it allows us to feel emotion so that we can move away or protect ourselves as necessary. It stores every memory you have ever had (by subject, as per the Gestalt way of thinking) or on a timeline (used in QTT). It is the seat of your emotions where the feelings attached to stored memories also exist.

Other things the Subconscious mind does

- Represses memories and if they are extremely traumatic, will not release them to us, until we are ready and able to deal with them. This is a protective mechanism and is designed for our own good.
- Strives to follow instructions from the conscious mind whilst looking for references to deem your values and beliefs true. Good if these beliefs are positive, not so good if they are negative.

- Puts meaning on filtered information recorded initially through the five senses (sight, smell, taste, touch and hearing) and passes this perception on to the conscious mind and is responsible for creating automatic behaviour. This behaviour can become a habit, especially if actions are repeated e.g. driving a car. It saves time if we don't have to think through each step every time we are doing something as automatic as changing gears.
- It is always striving to possess more knowledge.
- Importantly, it does not process negative thoughts directly but does this in a two-step process. So, positive goals and affirmations are more effective by being stated in a positive way. A goal such as "I want to get fit", as opposed to "I don't want to be unfit", is preferable as you don't have to firstly visualise being unfit and then visualising the second step, of getting fit. The positive statement is processed in a one-step, quicker manner. Concentrating on what you want to do in a positive way is therefore more effective.

Some of the behavioural patterns we have stored in our subconscious may not serve us and they may not even be based on reality. Instead they are based upon the meaning that our subconscious has attributed to them. For example, a child singing may be told continually to keep quiet and stop making a noise, which in turn may lead the child to feel ashamed and stop singing. Every time an even slightly negative reference is then made to the child singing, this will be reinforced negatively within the child's subconscious. Eventually the child believes that they are no good at singing and they feel embarrassed. In this way, an emotion of shame or guilt may also be attached to the memories of previously singing and that then becomes an embedded belief. The child believes that they cannot sing.

We understand that the subconscious part of our brain has the main function of protecting us. The subconscious will warn the child to avoid the pain previously felt at the times of ridicule when singing, if there is a chance of this happening again. A subconscious belief pattern will be setup that results in even the mere mention of singing, to a now older child, will trigger the negative memory and associated feelings of shame and hurt that the child encountered all those years ago. This is a warning to the child not to expose themselves to this hurtful situation again. So now they will not feel comfortable singing. In fact, they may now fully believe that they are no good at singing, even if they are gifted with a beautiful singing voice.

This is a small example, but many such patterns are setup, without even our being aware of them. These patterns run time and time again within our subconscious. Some patterns serve us well and others don't and instead limit us and hold us back. Consequently, we don't leave our comfort zones and don't challenge ourselves to reach our full potential. We can be "effectively stuck" and unable to move forward in life.

The behavioural patterns result from the beliefs and values that we have absorbed, especially in our young formative years (up until the age of eight years is the UNICEF definition) from our main influencers such as parents, guardians, siblings, friends and teachers. These are just some of the people that formed such a large and influential part of our young lives and in turn have a huge influence on our adult lives. To be able to progress both personally and professionally so that we can live the happy and satisfying lives that we are all entitled to, the first crucial step is to make ourselves aware of what exactly are our values and beliefs. Importantly, we must also identify the embedded patterns and self-limiting beliefs. Much like understanding why the little child does not believe that they could sing and being embarrassed about singing as a result. Once we break down the underlying causes, the belief can be shifted. Beliefs are not set in stone nor are they facts.

Deep self-knowledge is therefore the starting point in our journey. Self-knowledge begins with looking inside ourselves and identifying our values, beliefs and if possible, our negative subconscious patterns or (as I found out), using the services of a good coach is a great help.

Identifying Values, Beliefs and Subconscious Patterns

Our values are those attributes that we hold most dearly such as honesty, integrity, safety, loyalty, compassion and many more. These values have all been shaped by our specific experiences and through our many influencers, especially in the "Imprint Period" of the first eight years of our lives. The influencers could be family, friends, school or even the country or culture we live in, economics, media, religious or institutional factors.

Beliefs are opinions and convictions that we hold about our life or world. We have chosen to assign certain meanings to them and believe them to be true, even if they are not. Both values and beliefs influence our behaviour and success in life. Our subconscious minds have made sense of the past experiences and influences we were subjected to. By assigning meanings and emotions to them, it helps create our model of how we understand the world. The resulting models may not even be logically correct. These models of the world are what guide our behaviour and outlook on life. Even within the same family the belief that one child puts on a situation or event can be quite different to the beliefs that their siblings hold.

11

A belief starts as an opinion, a notion if you like, and then if repeated (e.g. "you are stupid"), may prompt the child to believe that it must be true. When the child decides that it is true and the subconscious searches and finds other corroborating references, the belief is reinforced, until it becomes a firm conviction. Alternatively, other beliefs can be empowering and assist the child, such as "you are intelligent", which boosts their confidence and they are more positively open to enjoying, learning and doing well at school. The belief is reinforced every time the child has another success in school.

A crucial point to note in all of this is that whether the belief is true or not, or as Henry Ford expressed it, "whether you believe you can or you can't, you are right" because the belief directly impacts on our behaviour. Negative ones disempower us whilst positive beliefs empower us. Notice winning sportspeople – they believe they can win and they do. If they don't believe they can do it – they certainly will not. They need to be in a positive frame of mind to perform well and to win. This applies to every area of our lives, not just in sport but also in our personal relationships, careers and in business.

EXERCISE:

List your "values and your beliefs" and then prioritise them as objectively as you can. If you are embarking on this journey with a friend, you can give each other feedback on your own perceptions of the list. The friend can serve as a more objective, outside observer. Sometimes we may be unaware of a belief or value that we hold to be especially important. This examination of values and beliefs and the priority that we hold them in, could also be done with the assistance of a coach.

A coach who establishes the right level of rapport with you, can ask the necessary, relevant and probing questions to dig deeply and determine whether your priorities are genuinely the same as you think they are.

EXERCISE:

Then do this exercise, "evaluate all the areas in your life" to see how content you are with each. You can score from 1–5 (5 is excellent, 4 is very good, 3 is good, 2 is unsatisfactory and 1 is very unsatisfactory). It can be done generally and for each major area of your life as follows:

1. Generally
2. Family

3. Relationships
4. Career
5. Health and fitness
6. Spirituality
7. Personal growth

Within each area above, you can dig deeper and list the specific items that are causing the low or high score. You are now identifying the areas where there is scope for improvement and the areas which you genuinely enjoy. The first step in establishing where change may be needed is to specifically identify the areas causing dissatisfaction. You can then move forward to looking at possibilities, goals and action plans to effect the change that you want. Also consider any self-limiting beliefs that you hold. I have explored these further in the next section.

Identifying Self-Limiting Beliefs

When doing the above exercise, note down any negative beliefs about yourself that make you feel uncomfortable. Just as in the case of the little child singing, are there any beliefs that make you feel in some way inadequate? It is very common for people to have these negative, limiting beliefs, so it would be unusual if you do not have any!

Several adults have carried negative messages with them throughout their lives e.g. I am not clever enough, I am too old, too lazy, too fat, not good-looking enough, the list is endless! They all, however, cause people to hold back from doing certain things that they might otherwise enjoy, resulting in them not achieving their full potential.

As stated previously, our subconscious mind is only trying to protect us and in doing so warns us when there are any situations that in the past have bad memories and feelings associated with them. The belief is therefore the meaning that we subconsciously chose to ascribe to the situation. That little child may be a wonderful singer, but her parents or siblings may have been tired and stressed and they just wanted peace. Beliefs are fine so long as they are not holding us back from reaching our full potential, as in stopping the little child from joyfully singing again.

It is important that when you do the exercise on beliefs, that you also pay attention to the negative ones that limit you. For you, it may be not learning new languages out of a negative self-belief you are no good at languages. It could be believing that you are no good at science. Other examples may include not applying for a promotion at work, as again, you don't feel good enough, not joining sports clubs or attending social occasions. The list of self-limiting beliefs is very long, and the mental blocks associated with them are unnecessary, usually incorrect, as well as being unhelpful.

The good thing about this exercise is that once we identify self-limiting beliefs, we can shift them and replace them with beliefs that do serve us. We will deal with a technique for shifting self-limiting beliefs that do not serve us, later in this chapter and in a more detailed manner, in Chapter 3.

Identifying Possibilities Using Vision Boards as a First Step to Goal Setting

Vision boards allow us to jot down our visions in whatever manner we wish. They are basically boards where you can write down your own words, inspirational quotes, insert or pin photos and pictures of things that you would love to do. It is not important whether you believe you can do them or not. By imagining freely, in such an uninhibited way, you are not limiting yourself (either consciously or subconsciously) before you even begin. Sometimes when we set goals, our subconscious is self-limiting us. even if we are not aware of it. The goals, therefore, may be restricted to certain areas of our life. The Vision Board can be a first step to formulating many goals that you would not ordinarily imagine you could achieve.

You may long to do some travelling to far-flung parts of the world but will limit yourself by saying you have no money and need to work, so you immediately discount it. However, you can still have it as a possibility on your vision board, maybe to do at a later stage in your life. Don't dismiss it though as it is part of your vision and your vision is very important.

The good thing about vision boards is that they allow your imagination and creativity to flow uninhibitedly and you may suddenly realise that there are things that you really would love to do at some point. It is important to keep them in mind. These are the things that will bring hope, knowledge, experience, maybe money and more satisfaction into your life when you achieve them.

We only have one life and regrets (about NOT doing things, rather than things that have been done) are all too frequent on death beds, as many studies carried out in nursing homes have revealed. When you have examined this area honestly and deeply, you can represent visually what you have learned about yourself and your visions. You may also find that it is an extremely enjoyable experience to create a vision board. At least I found it to be so, despite having had some reservations at first.

Now that you have a visual representation of what your ideal vision is, you can then look more realistically at the possibilities and begin to think about setting your own personal and professional goals. The ideal period for you to achieve your goals could be one year for example, it is entirely up to you. Another important thing to remember is that the vision board is your vision and just as your vision can and does change, so too can your vision board.

EXERCISE – Creating your own Vision Board and use of a Daily Journal to help with this process

The longest part of this exercise is to dream and think openly as to what your innermost thoughts and dreams actually are. By looking at the two previous exercises you can get an indication of what values are important to you, what areas of your life you are least content with and can see where your beliefs might be hindering you from making progress in these areas. When you review your results from those exercises, you have a basis for thinking about your vision board.

If you use a daily journal, you can note down ideas in this or use post-it stickers. You can even draw mind-maps as the ideas occur to you. I always used mind-maps throughout my life when trying to work out my plans, even when I didn't know what mind-maps were! Have yourself in the centre of the map and then have arrows coming out from you regarding all areas e.g. career, family, self-fulfilment, and health. In fact, include any area that you wish to choose. Then jot down alternative paths or options beneath each of these main areas.

Keeping a daily journal is a great practice and can be done first thing in the morning to list what's on your mind. My dreams from the previous night's sleep often give me a good indication if some ideas are brewing or even if something is bothering me. The journal can also be used for planning the day ahead, in broad brushstrokes (not meticulous detail) and for jotting down your ideas, future dreams or whatever you are thinking about. Gradually, these ideas, dreams and plans or strategies that perhaps have always been lurking at the back of your mind, will emerge. Previously, you may have dismissed the ideas as unrealistic, too expensive, too time-consuming, not good enough or one-hundred-and-one other excuses! Easy to do – so don't be too hard on yourself!

It is an excellent idea to think about each of the major areas in your life when starting to create your vision board too. You may have visions or aspirations about career, relationships, family, travel, hobbies, interests, finances, health and fitness, gardening, building a house, writing a book – or anything that you care about. You can use inspirational quotes, pieces of texts, photos, pictures, drawings, paint scenes or basically anything that symbolises your visions. I used a photo I took of "Dove Cottage" where the poet Wordsworth lived and wrote most of his poetry, in the beautiful Lake District in the UK, as a symbol of my desire to write. It is a truly beautiful cottage but is also a powerful and inspiring symbol. At the time of including Dove Cottage on my Vision Board, I would never have believed that not only would I start writing again but that I would write a book!

These items for your vision board can be arranged in any way you wish and as creatively as you want. It may take a few weeks to think everything through, but it does not have to be in detail. This is the initial creative process of identifying the vision before you start putting down the images, photos, drawings or quotes on to your vision board.

I find the process of creating a vision board to be an incredibly uplifting exercise and it clarified a lot of areas that I had been mentally tinkering with but did not have an action plan with which to follow through on. I would thoroughly recommend that you take the time out to think, note down the ideas as they come to you and then enjoy collecting and collating all your images, quotes, pictures on to your vision board. These may change as time passes but that is fine and is the way of life as you progress, grow and different visions and dreams assume different importance.

From performing this exercise, which is essentially a creative one, using the right-hand side of your brain, you can then filter (using the logical left-hand side of your brain) to identify what your goals might be for the short, medium or long-term.

By allowing ourselves the freedom to delve into our creativity in doing this vision board exercise, we are not automatically limiting the aspirations and visions in any way. When we set goals, be they in a personal or work capacity, we have automatically set limits, unknown to ourselves. This exercise of creating a vision board, frees up our mind by allowing it to dream freely and is very insightful into what we really want out of our life to help us to be happier and more satisfied people. The visual images also become imprinted into our subconscious therefore alerting it, so it can be more tuned in to opportunities and possibilities around those visions.

It is probably best to put the vision board in a more private space rather than exposing your dreams to negative comments from people who are more resistant and cynical to the idea of expressing visions creatively. This will be particularly unhelpful to you at this early stage of your journey. Perhaps place it in a bedroom, your office or work space at home, if you have one, rather than the living room where everyone has access to view it. It is *your* personal vision. You do not have to justify your vision or yourself to anyone.

You can look at the vision board daily to remind yourself of what life can potentially hold in store for you. Positive affirmations, visualisations and associating yourself into the vision board so you feel that you achieve the visions are very effective tools. (More on this in Chapter 4). I have linked in my personal goals to some of the images that are on my own vision board. It helped me hugely to dig deep into what I really wanted. After all, we only have one life, so we owe it to ourselves to make the most out of it. So much has changed in my life in the last two years and the goals are all nicely slotting into place and being achieved. More importantly, my lifestyle and way of thinking have also improved.

Identifying Personal and Professional Needs and Goals

If you do partake in the surprisingly enjoyable and creative exercise of creating a vision board, you can now take a step back and see what is more realistically achievable as a shorter-term goal. Obviously, this may not include extreme goals such as climbing Mount Everest, but it may include beginning to learn a language. This possibility can become a personal goal. Perhaps you visit Spain and have picked up a few words on holiday and would like to learn Spanish. The ideal situation is when some of your personal goals can be combined with some of your work or professional goals. Regarding climbing Mount Everest, this too is achievable but will require a more detailed plan incorporating fitness and medical aspects in addition to the logistics. You can begin learning a language in the short-term but climbing Mount Everest would obviously be a longer-term goal.

To take this learning Spanish example further, if the company you are working for has markets in Spain or better still, is trying to break into new markets in South America, it may also be in the company's interests that you or other employees learn Spanish. By stating this as one of your personal goals outside of work, it may be possible to also incorporate this goal on your work Personal Development Plan (as one of your work objectives). You may even get the sponsorship from work to undertake a

Spanish course or if there is a big drive for employees to learn Spanish, your company may arrange Spanish lessons in-house at your workplace.

Clearly, most of your personal goals will not be the same as your work or professional goals but where there is overlap, this is doubly effective. Most people would like to be promoted and to do so, should be considering attending relevant training courses, learning new languages and gaining more work experience (either inside or outside the company). All activities are relevant to your successful career progression. By gaining promotion, it will also benefit your self-esteem, your CV going forward (should you wish to change companies in the future) or even help gain promotion within your existing company.

Promotion should mean you will earn more money and receive more benefits such as healthcare, pension, shares, bonus and many more. It will help serve as a positive role model for your children and family who will learn from you and be proud that you have been successful in a challenging career or in business. It is satisfying to realise that your ability and efforts are being rewarded and this is a great lesson for them to learn. It is also a great lesson for you to learn that you can be such a good role model and affirmation that you are indeed a capable, highly regarded, valued, professional or business person.

EXERCISE: State your goals for the coming year, maybe by using the guidelines below.

7 ways of effectively setting goals include:

1. **Stating each goal as a positive statement, written down precisely, to crystallise and reinforce it**. This is also important so that you set up the goal to give the best opportunity for positive manifestation (see the next section on "Manifestation and the Law of Attraction"). It is vitally important to *feel* it – so that it is not just an empty sentence – but something that you genuinely care about. So, create a compelling outcome for what you want and feel what it would be like when you achieve that goal.

2. **Ensuring high priority goals**. Pick goals that you really care about and want to achieve as opposed to goals that someone else wants you to achieve.

3. **Goals should be realistic**. If you want to learn something new, then that is admirable, but it must be something that you can realistically achieve. Maybe you want to start walking as an activity but if you

want to walk the entire "Camino Way" in Southern France and Northern Spain (a route that pilgrims used to travel on their way to the Compostela de Santiago), then ensure that you work your fitness up to this level and do not attempt it straight away. My cousin did the entire walk over several years, as her holidays permitted and by doing one stage each time. She also walks regularly in her life therefore it was realistic. I considered doing the Camino walk but realised that I do not enjoy long walks even though I would like to see that part of the world and love Spain. It was a fanciful rather than a realistic goal, so I dropped it.

4. **Set "performance" goals over which you have control rather than "outcome" goals.** Outcome goals are those over which you may *not* have control but are more dependent upon other people. If the goal is not achieved for reasons outside of your control, you may then feel disheartened if you don't succeed, even though it was through no fault of your own. Performance goals are better as you do have more control over these and a higher likelihood of success as a result.

5. **Goals should be self-initiated and self-maintained i.e. done primarily for you and that you take responsibility for it.** If it is something that someone else wants you to do and you are not particularly keen and do not own it, there is less chance of you achieving it. This links in with setting high-priority goals in item 2.

6. **Verifying that the goal is OK? Ask yourself the questions below:**

    a.   What will happen if you achieve it?
    b.   What will happen if you don't achieve it?
    c.   What won't happen if you achieve it?
    d.   What won't happen if you don't achieve it?

If the goal results in you having to move to a different country, will this suit your family and children's schooling needs? Maybe.

7. **Remembering that your goals should be SMART i.e.**

S = Specific (who, what, where, when - rather than vagueness).

M = Measurable (how much, how many, how often, by when).

A = Attainable (learn from others. Do you have the necessary resources and/or how to access them? If you are unfit and want to run a 10k marathon – gradual training will be necessary and maybe a medical check first, depending upon your circumstances and fitness).

R = Realistic (look at your personal history – scale your goals down if you have a history of not achieving them in the past. Scale up if you have had a successful history).

T = Timeline (if there is no deadline, then consciously and subconsciously you will feel no urgency or compelling reason to try and achieve your goals. It is better to let your physical and energetic body know what to do and when).

An example of a SMART goal might be: "I am going to get fit by exercising and running three times a week and will run a 10k marathon in June. I will feel more energetic, fit more easily into my size 12 clothes and look and feel more confident, toned and healthy for my summer holidays". Contrast that goal with "I will get fit". In a work situation, specific metrics can be used. "Reduce month-end closing time to two working days by June", being one for the finance team.

Corporate and Personal Goals

Setting your goals in a corporate or work environment – as distinct from the vision board scenario – entails you being aware of some of your direct manager's goals as well as the overall corporate goals of the company for which you work. It is important from a promotional viewpoint that you are aware of what your manager's goals are so that you can assist the manager to achieve them. This will place you in a more realistic and favourable position for promotion. It may be that your manager is promoted within the company and their previous role becomes vacant. Alternatively, if they move on with a different company, then their position will also become vacant. If you have proved your worth as a supportive team player, then this should be reflected in favourable annual reviews and should assist you in gaining promotion and climbing the corporate ladder, if that is what you want. Even success in applying for roles in other companies, if they are a better fit for your career progression and lifestyle, will be enhanced by this approach.

If you formulate your goals for work in the absence of what your manager and indeed your company are striving to achieve, then the goals that you set will be less effective and will not be aligning up as well as they could. This does not serve you or the company. A good manager will know this but do not be afraid to request this information and explain that you want to align your goals as best as possible with both your manager's goals and the corporate goals, to contribute in the most effective way possible. Not every manager is a good one, so never be afraid to show initiative, be proactive and explain objectively why you are approaching your own goal setting in this way.

Manifestation and Law of Attraction

The concept of "Manifestation" is not one that usually sits comfortably beside discussions on Corporate Goals. It is still held under suspicion by some. However, it basically relates to the law of attraction (as identified by Einstein who was no fluffy-headed thinker himself) and is based upon the fact that energy vibrates at distinct levels and that energies vibrating at similar levels are attracted to each other.

If you think about all the good stuff that has happened to date in your life and then the adversities or misfortunes that people encounter generally (except in cases where fate or natural disasters such as earthquakes intervene), they are normally the result of the choices and decisions that we have all made at some level, at some time. What you manifest today – be it all or some of a car, house, family, career, health, happiness, wealth – did not happen purely by chance. You manifested it by your decisions, efforts, input and energy. Manifestation to be truly effective requires that you are vibrating positive energy at a high frequency.

Emotions that vibrate at a low frequency such as jealousy, shame and guilt also attract similarly low vibrational results.

Whilst this theory may seem a bit out there at first, think of two pianos in a room. The note middle C is struck on one piano and without any other interference or input, the other piano vibrates at the same frequency, at the middle C note. This is a very insightful example and puts a more scientific basis on the Law of Attraction, clearly showing that what we give out (energy-wise) then we attract back – be it in our relationships, career, health or finances.

Einstein famously said: "Everything is energy, that is all there is to it. Match the frequency of the reality you want, and you cannot help but get that reality. It can be no other way. This is not philosophy, this is physics."

Much research has been done into the area of Quantum Physics and Quantum Science – so for the remaining cynics amongst you, I will refer you to some further reading:

- Max Planck founder of *Quantum Theory* and Nobel Prize winner for this work in 1991.
- *Quantum Physics Consciousness Science* by David Albert PhD.
- *Quantum Physics and Consciousness* by Amit Goswami PhD.
- *Consciousness and Superstring Unified Field Theory* by John Hagelin PhD.
- *Power Vs Force* by David Hawkins MD PhD.
- *The Divine Matrix* by Gregg Braden.
- Deepak Chopra's extensive body of work.

Given that we accept the Law of Attraction on some level and therefore manifestation, it makes absolute sense that we will all live happier, more fulfilled and balanced lives if we manifest positively and abundantly. Abundance also brings in the idea that we should give not just to get but be aware of being comfortable with giving and receiving "more than enough".

Now match up your goals to see if they align with your vision board. Revisit your vision board and goals frequently to remind yourself to keep on track. Set mini-milestones if necessary.

Relax and set off on the journey. Approach this with confidence, so you vibrate at a higher frequency and attract the same back. It is much more rewarding to approach life from a positive place rather than from a place of fear and lack. If you are giving out lower vibrations, then this will attract similar low vibrations to you in return and this does not serve you.

Replacing Negative Beliefs with Empowering Beliefs

As we touched upon earlier in this chapter, everyone holds values and beliefs and undoubtedly some of those beliefs will be negative. The beliefs are purely meanings that our subconscious mind has assigned to past experiences. If they cause negative feelings in us, then more than likely, some beliefs will be holding us back from achieving our full potential. They are not facts but only meanings that we decided to assign to them and to associate certain memories and emotions to them. Therefore, we can explore those negative, disempowering beliefs and expose them for what they are. Then we can shift them and replace them with empowering beliefs.

In QTT – a modality developed and taught by Moira Geary – there are several techniques available to release emotions related to negative beliefs that through time became embedded neural pathways. In doing this release on emotions, we can change behaviours by shifting the negative beliefs. Just as importantly as releasing associated emotions, we can replace the old beliefs with new empowering beliefs that serve us better. We can additionally reconcile conflicting ideas and beliefs. These techniques which will be explored in more detail later in the book, include:

1. Basic Quantum Release – QTT Technique
2. Advanced Quantum Release – QTT Technique
3. Parts Integration – NLP Technique
4. Reframing – NLP Technique

There can also be further "polishing off techniques", which will be discussed in the next chapter. It is preferable to use a qualified QTT practitioner for these techniques as they will have a deeper and fuller understanding of your individual situation. They also possess the knowledge and experience of successfully using these techniques to best help their clients. It is important that you know the techniques can be successfully used and that you can get release on feelings attached to these emotions (probably held for many years), so that you can then move on freely without the need to keep carrying the painful baggage that is holding you back.

When you completed the exercise examining your values and beliefs earlier, you also understood the importance and value to yourself of identifying any negative, self-limiting beliefs that you personally hold. It will be hugely useful for you to identify and explore these self-limiting beliefs and try and shift them, using a friend or preferably a coach who has trained in QTT and NLP. I can personally vouch that the techniques have worked on me (and on others that I have practiced on) and we have all greatly benefitted from the experience of releasing trapped emotions and memories and replacing negative, disempowering beliefs with positive, empowering ones.

The key for any of the QTT or NLP techniques to work is that there must be a good rapport between the coach and the client. The questioning by the coach should be powerful, digging deep into the crux of the matter and identifying the real reasons that caused the client to assign the negative meaning in the first place. These negative beliefs influence our behaviour causing the subsequent embedded thought and behaviour patterns that have not served us but have held us back so that we remain "stuck". To assist with building rapport, it is useful to understand about internal representational systems.

There are various types of "internal representational" systems in NLP that are discussed in the next section. By understanding the different types of ways in which people perceive the world, we can understand and communicate better with them. There are verbal and non-verbal traits or body language associated with each of the types of Internal Representational system.

Another way to communicate effectively with people is to observe body language generally and be aware of any physiological changes that a person exhibits. This could be shifts in skin colour, skin tone, depth and rapidity of breathing or dilation of pupils. All these physiological changes are very relevant body language indicators. The coach can work more effectively with the client if they understand what is going on at a deeper, subconscious level by noting their body language. Careful observation, listening and asking relevant, probing questions allows the coach to enable the client to identify "blocks", understand them and come to their own conclusions. Changes can then be made to move forward in a more positive way. The coach can assist in the process so that within the client, both the conscious and subconscious minds come into harmony and agreement on the "belief change" that has occurred. The coach is merely a channel in this process.

When we are at our most basic level and operating from a place of fear, our behaviour becomes needy. We can appreciate that alternatively, we can choose to come from a place of positivity or "love" where our motivation is moving forward and is not based on fear. QTT has explored the basic needs and how we express ourselves with body language and Moira Geary has identified seven behavioural codes to help explain what exactly is going on. This enables deeper understanding and ultimately benefits people, enabling them to live fuller and more joyous lives. QTT recognises that coming from a positive place serves us so much better.

In the next chapter, we shall explore the seven basic behavioural codes of QTT in detail and the associated body language that we may express when there are fears within us surrounding these codes. The QTT techniques allow the fears to be released and for us to change embedded ways of thinking (neural pathways) to free that person from the negative mental blocks and the resulting negative behaviour.

The Main Internal Representational Systems

Everybody has a characteristic preferred "Internal Representational System". This means that they have their own way of viewing and experiencing the world within which they live. By understanding the representational system of ourselves and others, we can communicate better with them and can also control the way in which we interpret (or quite often, misinterpret!) things. Representational Systems are also called Modalities and are essentially the ways in which we "represent" the world, having received input through our five senses of seeing, hearing, touching, smelling and taste.

There are six basic "Internal Representational" systems (visual, auditory, kinaesthetic, olfactory, gustatory and auditory digital or "self-talk"). For the purposes of gaining initial understanding, we can identify the four main types below. A certified QTT or NLP Practitioner would have a much more in-depth knowledge and understanding of this whole area and can use this understanding to greater effect when working with clients.

(1) Visual i.e. seeing. You see the world and experience life events primarily in a visual way. Commonly using words such as "clear", "focused", "illuminate", "look", "picture" to describe what you experience or wish to do.

(2) Auditory i.e. hearing. You hear the world rather than see it. Commonly using words such as "be heard", "harmonise", "listen", "rings a bell", "tune in" in your language.

(3) Kinaesthetic i.e. feeling. Often using words such as "catch up", "grasp", "tap into", "throw out", "turn around" when describing events.

(4) Auditory Digital i.e. inner dialogue or self-talk. Using words such as "change", "consider", "experience", "motivate", "understand". More people are in this "category" than you would imagine, including me.

EXERCISE:

Try and work out your own Internal Representational System.

Use the examples given of Internal Representational Systems to assist you in this exercise. (Much more information is available on these "Internal Representational Systems" and a good NLP coach will have exercises which will readily highlight which type you most closely resemble).

Observe others and notice their language – both body and verbal – to see if you can understand their "Internal Representational Systems" too.

NLP developed a bad name in the 1970s, as it was being used quite aggressively as a sales tool when closing the sale was the only endgame and understanding and using body language was very cynically applied.

However, in this book I am selecting the parts of NLP that will help with building rapport and aiding better communication in a positive way – not so that you manipulate potential clients or customers to close every sale!

I was at a conference in Orlando, Florida and arrived the night that Donald Trump was elected. Interesting times! The conference was nothing to do with politics but was a speaking/sales/coaching mix where aggressive NLP techniques were blatantly being used on the audience. From a sales point of view, some results were achieved. (I didn't buy into their overly aggressive approach and I am normally open to ideas and purchasing products or services if I perceive there to be value in them). Clearly, the value of some of the products and services being sold was questionable in my view. To see the audience being worked upon using language (both body and verbal), gestures and tactics was interesting and educational. I think a lot of people got carried away on a tide of frenzied emotion and I spoke to several who as they "came down" regretted their choices.

However, just to clarify, I am not promoting NLP as a sales tool but as a beneficial communication tool.

We can now move on to exploring the seven behavioural codes of QTT in more detail and seeing how this can help us identify areas in our lives that may be lacking. We can then look to improve upon them.

Chapter 2

The Relevance of QTT Seven Behavioural Codes

Needs and Behavioural Codes

Moira Geary (Mind Experts' Academy) who developed the QTT modality has identified hundreds of behaviours in her work helping clients and has condensed these into behaviours driven by seven behavioural codes. In summary, all humans seek to be happy. "Needs" come into the equation when our ego or fears of not fulfilling the codes exist. To explain this further, I will reference Maslow and his famous hierarchy of needs developed back in 1943. This is a starting point in our understanding of human behaviour.

Maslow's "Hierarchy of Needs" starts by identifying the very basic need for safety and security and then progresses up to the higher needs of self-actualisation. I have reproduced an extract from an article explaining in more detail about Maslow's Hierarchy of Needs as this represents a very fundamental step in the development of our thinking around behaviour. This excellent article was written by Neel Burton M.D. in 2012.

Before looking at the article, it is useful to link the ideas behind Maslow's Hierarchy of Needs to QTT. Whilst QTT is developing the idea of the needs being identified and fulfilled, it then concentrates more heavily upon studying the behaviours that these needs drive. Again, the distinction is that the QTT codes and needs are very different. As mentioned, a "need" is coming from a fear that we will not achieve it. This is also very much the emphasis that Maslow concentrates upon. Alternatively, that which we are wishing to achieve e.g. security, can also be approached from a more positive angle. QTT views the behavioural code (rather than a need) from a more positive angle as the better approach.

Maslow's Hierarchy of Needs

Extract from article by Neel Burton:

Neel Burton M.D. Hide and Seek

Maslow's Hierarchy of Needs

Why true freedom is a luxury of the mind.

In his influential paper of 1943, *A Theory of Human Motivation*, the American psychologist Abraham Maslow proposed that healthy human beings have a certain number of needs, and that these needs are arranged in a hierarchy, with some needs (such as physiological and safety needs) being more primitive or basic than others (such as social and ego needs). Maslow's so-called 'hierarchy of needs' is often presented as a five-level pyramid, with higher needs coming into focus only once lower, more basic needs are met.

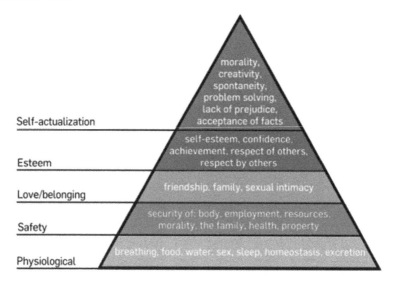

Maslow's Hierarchy of Needs

Maslow called the bottom four levels of the pyramid "deficiency needs" because a person does not feel anything if they are met and becomes anxious if they are not. Thus, physiological needs such as eating, drinking, and *sleeping* are deficiency needs, as are safety needs, social needs such as *friendship* and sexual intimacy, and ego needs such as *self-esteem* and recognition. In contrast, Maslow called the fifth level of the pyramid a "growth need" because it enables a person to "self-actualise" or reach his fullest potential as a human being. Once a person has met his deficiency needs, he can turn his attention to self-actualisation; however, only a small minority of people are able to self-actualise because self-actualisation requires uncommon qualities such as honesty, independence, awareness, objectivity, *creativity*, and originality.

Although Maslow's hierarchy of needs has been criticised for being overly-schematic and lacking in scientific grounding, it presents an intuitive and potentially useful theory of human motivation. After all, there is surely some grain of truth in the popular saying that one cannot philosophise on an empty stomach, and in Aristotle's early observation that "all paid work absorbs and degrades the mind".

Aristotle (right): 'Courage is the first of human qualities because it is the quality which guarantees the others.'

Once a person has met his deficiency needs, the focus of his *anxiety* shifts to self-actualisation and he begins – even if only at a *subconscious* or semiconscious level – to contemplate the context and meaning of life. He may come to *fear* that death is inevitable and that life is meaningless, but at the same time cling on to the cherished belief that his life is eternal or at least important. This gives rise to an inner conflict that is sometimes referred to as "existential anxiety" or, more colourfully, as "the *trauma* of non-being".

Existential anxiety is so disturbing that most people avoid it at all costs. They construct an inauthentic but comforting reality made up of *moral* codes, bourgeois values, habits, customs, culture, and even – arguably – *religion*. The Harvard theologian Paul Tillich (1886–1965) and indeed *Freud* himself suggested that religion is nothing more than a carefully crafted coping mechanism for existential anxiety. For Tillich, true faith consists simply in "being vitally concerned with that ultimate reality to which I give the symbolical name of God".

There are some very good points illustrated in the above article so hopefully it explains the themes of hierarchical needs more clearly.

The difference between *behaviour* and *needs* is important. Anything in life that becomes a need basically translates into something that you are afraid you are not going to have or get. In other words, you are coming from a place of fear. Clearly, it is better to be coming from a positive place of love (or from "positivity", if that word, resonates better with you) rather than from a place of fear because fear inhibits and blocks progress and manifestation. A behaviour that comes from a place of fear/lack is never the best choice – it is always far better to come from a place of love/positivity.

When we are fearful, we cannot be truly happy, despite the amazing resilience of the human spirit. The resilience can be seen especially in young children. Survivors of the holocaust and other tragic wars plus leaders such as Nelson Mandela are other notable examples. QTT stresses the view that by fulfilling the codes positively, people will be happier because they will be running and fulfilling their behavioural codes from a place of positivity rather than from a place of fear.

Letting go and releasing if there are any fears related to any of the seven Behavioural Codes is therefore very important. Before we examine the seven QTT Behavioural Codes, I want to draw attention to their link to the chakras. So first we will look at the chakras in more detail.

What are the Chakras?

There are one hundred and fourteen chakras existing in our body, but we will only deal with the seven main chakras in this book. Chakras are basically the main centres in our bodies through which energy flows. In a comparable way to our vascular system transporting blood throughout our body using a transport system of arteries and veins, energy travels throughout our body using a system of channels, known as meridians. This idea of energy flow, meridians, energy centres and energy being blocked is the basis of many Eastern healing treatments and therapies such as acupuncture, reiki and yoga.

There can be blockages in our heart, arteries or veins that hinder the free flow of blood through our vascular system and cause health problems. So too, there can be blockages (or imbalances) in our energy system. These energetic blockages or imbalances tend to manifest by causing emotional problems that can also have physical repercussions. Imbalances or blockages within our energy system are linked to our chakras which are the main energy centres within our bodies. See the following diagram:

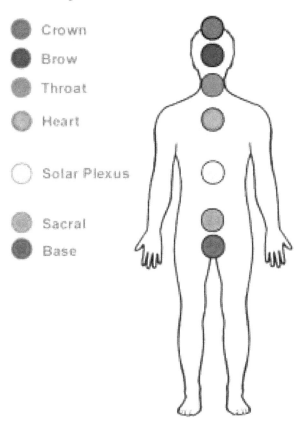

The body's seven main Chakras

- Crown
- Brow
- Throat
- Heart
- Solar Plexus
- Sacral
- Base

1. Root Chakra

This First (Root or Base) Chakra represents our foundation and relates to the feeling of being grounded. It is associated with the adrenal glands at the top of the kidneys (affecting kidneys, bladder, spine, muscle and bone).

- **Location:** At the base of the spine in the tailbone area.
- **Emotional issues:** Revolve around survival issues such as financial independence, money and food.
- **Associated Colour:** Red.
- **Associated Element:** Earth.

Healing Exercises:

- Stamping your bare feet on the ground. (Yes, I know it sounds childish – but sometimes we can learn from children!) The Root

Chakra is all about feeling "grounded"- so in that context, this exercise is not so outrageous.

- Practicing Kundalini Yoga i.e. the principle behind Kundalini yoga is that in freeing up this area at the base of the spine in the tailbone area, we can unleash the unlimited potential that lies within that energy centre. We can then open-up our lower spine. In the Kundalini form of yoga, there is a lot of core work on the abs area and around the spine with more sitting than usual.
- Bridge Pose is another good yoga pose to try and open-up the lower spine area.

Healing Foods:

- Red coloured foods like apples and beets.
- Hot spices like red cayenne peppers and Tabasco sauce.
- Vegetables from the ground like potatoes and carrots.
- Animal proteins like red meat and eggs.

2. Sacral Chakra

The Second (Sacral, Hara or Swadisthan) Chakra represents our connection and ability to accept others and new experiences. It relates to our ability to feel creative, sexual and to accept change. This chakra is associated with the gonads i.e. ovaries in women and testicles in men. It is the Centre of Stability, Feelings and Sexual Energy.

- **Location:** Lower abdomen, about 2 inches below the navel and 2 inches into our body.
- **Emotional issues:** Revolve around a sense of abundance, well-being, pleasure, sexuality.
- **Associated Colour:** Orange.
- **Associated Element:** Water.

HEALING EXERCISES:

- Pelvic thrusts.
- Cobra Yoga Pose.

Healing Foods:

- Orange coloured foods like oranges and tangerines.
- Nuts.

3. Solar Plexus Chakra

The Third (Solar Plexus or Manipura) Chakra represents our ability to be confident and in control of our lives. It is the Emotional Centre and is associated with the Pancreas (affecting liver, stomach and entire digestive tract). It is the Centre of Power, Wisdom and Emotions.

- **Location:** In the upper abdomen in the stomach area.
- **Emotional issues:** Self-worth, self-confidence and self-esteem.
- **Associated Colour:** Yellow.
- **Associated Element:** Fire.

HEALING EXERCISES:

- Kundalini Yoga: Boat Pose.
- Dancing. Especially shaking your hips.

Healing Foods:

- Yellow coloured foods like corn.
- Grains and fibre like granola and whole wheat bread.
- Teas like peppermint and chamomile tea.

4. Heart Chakra

The Fourth (Heart or Anahata) Chakra represents our ability to love. This involves the quality of our love, our past loves and our future loves. It is associated with the thymus gland (affecting heart, lungs and circulatory system). It is the Centre of Love and Compassion.

- **Location:** In the centre of the chest just above the heart.
- **Emotional issues:** Love, joy and inner peace.
- **Associated Colour:** Green.
- **Associated Element:** Air.

HEALING EXERCISES:

- Bikram Yoga.
- The most effective exercise is to simply open our hearts to others to open the Heart Chakra.

Healing Foods:

- Green coloured foods like leafy vegetables and spinach.
- Green tea.

5. Throat Chakra

The Fifth (Throat or Vishuddha) Chakra represents our ability to communicate and express ourselves regarding feelings, speaking the truth and holding secrets. It is associated with the thyroid gland (affecting lungs, throat and respiratory tract). It is the Centre of Communication and Self-Expression.

- **Location:** In the throat.
- **Emotional issues:** Communication, self-expression of feelings and the truth.
- **Associated Colour:** Blue.
- **Associated Element:** Sky.

HEALING EXERCISES:

- Shoulder stands.
- Singing, chanting.

Healing Foods:

- Juices and teas.
- All types of fruits.

6. Sixth Eye Chakra

The Sixth (Eye of Cobra or Ajna) Chakra represents our ability to focus on and see the big picture. Using intuition, imagination, wisdom and ability to think and make decisions as part of this process. It is associated with the pituitary (or master) gland (affecting eyes, hypothalamus and nervous system). It is the Seat of Intuition and Centre of Willpower.

- **Location:** Forehead between the eyes (also called the Chopra Chakra).
- **Emotional issues:** Intuition, imagination, wisdom and the ability to think and make decisions.
- **Associated Colour:** Indigo.

HEALING EXERCISES:

- Child's Pose or other types of yoga poses with forward bends.
- Eye exercises.
- Herbal oil treatment.

Healing Foods:

- Purple coloured fruits like grapes and blueberries.
- Chocolate.
- Lavender flavoured spices or tea.

7. Crown Chakra

The Seventh (Crown or Sahasrara) Chakra represents the highest chakra and our ability to be fully connected spiritually. It is associated with inner and outer beauty and in the highest form – true bliss. Its connection to the endocrine system is via the pineal gland which affects the cerebrum, which is the largest part of the human brain, associated with higher brain function such as thought and action. It is the Connection to the Higher Self.

- **Location:** At the very top of the head.
- **Emotional issues:** Inner and outer beauty, our connection to spirituality and pure bliss.
- **Associated Colour:** Violet.

HEALING EXERCISES:

- **Meditation.**
- **Running or cardio.**

Healing Foods: Since this Crown Chakra represents our spiritual connection to our surroundings, this chakra does not benefit from healing foods. This chakra is more likely to benefit from breathing clean, fresh air and sunshine.

Now that we have considered each of the chakras and what they represent, we can look at and link the above chakras to the Seven Behavioural Codes of QTT.

Below is the diagram again, showing the location of the chakras within our body.

The body's seven main Chakras

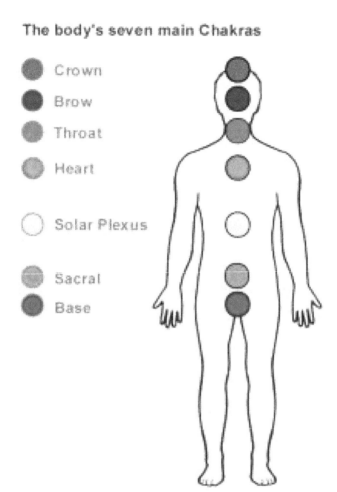

Crown

Brow

Throat

Heart

Solar Plexus

Sacral

Base

Blocked energy in any of our seven chakras can often lead to illness, as we all instinctively realise at some level. We have more than likely noticed that negative people do tend to get sicker and recover more slowly than positive people. It is very important to understand what each chakra represents and what we can do to keep this energy flowing freely. I have a science degree and am a qualified accountant, FCCA, so am a relatively logical thinker and would not endorse such a notion if I did not believe that there was some logical basis or truth in it. I have given a very quick summary of the seven main chakras earlier and now will consider how I believe they link into our thoughts, feelings, behaviour and then linking that into the seven QTT Behavioural Codes. Before we look at this area, there are some other points to consider.

Moira Geary first noted that these seven Behavioural Codes of QTT are related to the energy of the chakras. Discomfort associated with the area in the body where the chakras are located is a key principle within QTT. Moira discovered this by observing hundreds of clients and noticing how they spoke with their hands. They were subconsciously indicating the areas in their bodies where they were feeling the emotional discomfort.

These feelings of discomfort were linked to embedded ways that the clients were thinking. Another way to express it is to describe it as neural pathways that had been set up earlier in their lives. The repetition of the thought and the associated feelings became embedded within the person.

Someone feeling that they were not being heard or listened to would unconsciously point to their throat during sessions with Moira. This area of the body, the "Throat Chakra" and the imbalance being felt in it by the client provides an indication of where the root of the problem may lie.

The chakras are therefore aligned to the QTT Behavioural Codes and once we are aware of this link, then we can read the body language to see where the problems lie physically and where the beliefs and associated emotions may need to be released. This is a very fundamental principle in understanding QTT.

Before any techniques are used, it is vital that we have explored, investigated and thoroughly understood the issues (and associated blocked emotions and energy) by deep questioning and communication with the person affected by it.

We can also use this understanding (gained through the deep dive questioning and communication) to see if a technique e.g. the Quantum Release Technique has worked. If the discomfort previously felt e.g. in the throat no longer exists, when the client is asked to think again about the situation that caused the discomfort, then if no discomfort is now felt, the technique has been successful.

If it has not worked, then further deep questioning and communication will be done to ensure that the real root causes have been identified. As you would expect, the success of the questioning and communication requires good rapport and trust between the coach and client. It is also essential to appreciate if there are further repercussions and if the course of action is really the best way to go i.e. "ecologically correct".

In my own situation, it worked – and I was released from a problem that I have had for many years and the emotions surrounding it. That is why I feel so strongly that people can benefit from QTT knowledge and techniques. Again, perhaps better if done by a qualified coach, trained in QTT. Personally, I paid a large amount of money, previously, to another coach for whom I did several exercises and work and who did not use any QTT techniques. Despite my huge engagement and resolve, it was plainly no use. I learned a good lesson from that. This QTT stuff really does work – and works quickly. It is especially effective when used with NLP and Life Coaching Techniques.

If you are like me – and I believe that I am logical and analytical (and have been cynical about some holistic practices) – you may choose not to accept what I am sharing. Naturally, that's fine, but I do know that I was not enjoying life, despite everything apparently being in place. The benefits of having good health – for both myself and family, a good education, successful career with high earnings and a lovely home - still did not bring me happiness or fulfilment. We had bought a field in the country and built a house, with space and freedom for ourselves, children, cats and dogs. We have grown lots of plants, trees and bushes. I have grown organic strawberries commercially and successfully and there is a small stream which still provides pleasure for my family including my now adult children and for the animals. This was everything I had ever wanted so why was something missing from my life? I was looking for something new after thirty-eight years working in Accountancy. I took some time out to learn golf, write, travel, play tennis again, continue with my Spanish – but there was still something blocking my enjoyment.

Frequently being in the company of negative or occasionally, toxic people and situations, colours everyone's perception and enjoyment of life. This may occur at work, in your personal life or it may even occur in both. Even though we understand that perception is not reality, it is felt and experienced by our brain just as powerfully as if it were reality. This was the underlying reason for my discontent and my block.

For me to enjoy my life more fully, things had to change. They did. I understood, let go of the emotions associated with the memories and automatically my perception, actions and reactions changed. What had specifically changed?

In my personal life, I had occasionally been at the receiving end of negative comments regarding being born in England (as I am living in Ireland) and there was some regular begrudgery coming from the same source that caused me disquiet and even hurt at one stage. My behaviour towards the perpetrators had always been to help them as my services as an accountant were frequently requested but this rapidly turned into a pattern where I was being used and manipulated on several levels. I could see that it was unreasonable. It was only when I totally understood and recognised the behaviours, their causes and released on them (during a Quantum Release method performed by Moira Geary), that I was free from all the discomfort and baggage. I also realised that some people should be side-lined in your life if they are innately negative, drain your energy and are always seeking to use you for their own purposes with no reciprocal give. It also doesn't help if they belittle your achievements, assign them to someone else and make regular, snide remarks aimed at putting you down to make themselves feel more important. Ring any bells?!

This can and does happen in many work situations, as I am sure many of you are all too familiar with. The work situations I seemed to be able to handle better, probably because I was accustomed to being objective and professional in a work environment. Having said that, I did decide to finally leave corporate life after becoming increasingly dissatisfied with the long hours, particularly the eternal struggle to take my holidays and then the death of a close friend's sister in the UK and the thoughts of not being able to go to her funeral, clinched it for me. What was genuinely important to me? Was it really the constant churning out financial statements and figures to meet deadlines or was it about the people I loved and cared for and enjoying my life and my holidays?

I did not expect to experience such sustained negative behaviour within my personal life, however, but as it had also happened earlier on in my life there probably was an embedded pathway lurking beneath the surface as well. I am now very keenly aware that it regularly happens to so many people because of several conversations I have had. The good news is that the situation can be turned around entirely. I was that soldier! It is hugely satisfying to now be able to help lift the worries and the pain off another person's shoulders so that they can leave the baggage behind and carry on positively with their lives, unimpeded.

It is essential to understand that our thoughts impact our emotions and therefore our moods. Our moods in turn affect our behaviour and ultimately our results. Negative thoughts that we receive externally from others may eventually become internalised if repeated enough times. Eventually, we internally develop our own negative self-talk. This will bring your mood and energy level right down and serves no useful purpose. If you start to be more aware of your thoughts and identify any negative patterns – then ask yourself three questions:

1. Is it logical?
2. Is it real?
3. Does it serve me?

This will help you to look more objectively at the reality of the situation rather than your own negative perception. You can decide to change your negative thoughts. By doing this you can change your mood and lighten your spirits, increasing the level of the energy that you are vibrating at. To manifest positively, we appreciate and accept that we need to be vibrating at higher frequencies so that we attract the same. By dwelling in the emotions of guilt or shame (which have the lowest vibrations) you will vibrate at the lowest frequencies and attract similar back. Anyone who tries to manipulate you into feeling guilt or shame for their own purposes is to be avoided. I have cut out or minimised contact with such people.

We can now examine briefly, the link between different chakras and the seven behavioural codes in Quantum Thinking Technologies. You will notice that the chakra concept is very much tied into yoga as well as the link to Maslow's Hierarchy of Needs.

Link between Chakras and the Seven Behavioural Codes of QTT.

The main difference between the chakras and the QTT Behavioural Codes is that QTT uses the knowledge of the chakras and develops further the idea that our behaviours are driven to fulfil the attributes of the chakras. The chakras can be used to identify where a person has an imbalance in those areas so can pinpoint where work and possibly a release of emotions and a shift in thinking needs to be addressed. Other therapies also use the chakras to identify problem areas requiring energy work in the case of reiki and acupuncture. Both are very ancient Eastern holistic treatments acknowledging the importance of energy and holistic healing as opposed to the more chemical approach to healing used in mainstream Western medicine.

In summary, Maslow's Hierarchy of Needs was explored and developed further by linking these "needs" (a negative connotation) to a more "positive" behavioural code as set out in QTT. This in turn ties into understanding the chakras to diagnose where the client is feeling the physical discomfort or even pain in their body and delve further into the background reasons.

The body's seven main Chakras

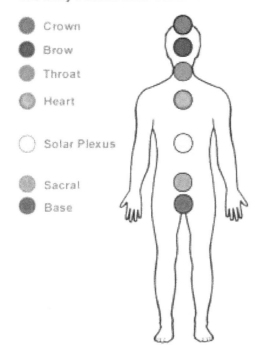

- Crown
- Brow
- Throat
- Heart
- Solar Plexus
- Sacral
- Base

I have reproduced the QTT seven Behavioural Codes below and have colour coded them to relate them to the corresponding chakras in the diagram above. There are many similarities in the seven codes to the corresponding chakras.

Code 7 – CONNECTION   No separation, belonging, connecting to.

Code 6 – EVOLUTION   Growth and progression.

Code 5 – AUTHENTIC VOICE: Speaking your truth, being authentic.

Code 4 – LOVE: Self-love, giving and receiving love.

– IMPORTANCE: Relevance, identity, raised self-esteem.

Code 2 – DIVERSITY: Creativity, selection and risk.

Code 1 – SURENESS: Survival, safety.

Code 1 – SURENESS: Survival and safety

QTT code 1 will lead to behaviours to fulfil basic needs – survival and safety e.g. a place to live, food etc. As we evolve in our own lives, we want more from life than just to exist. Different people may not want much more than basic needs, however, most of us, given the chance, want to evolve and grow. That is also why it is so important not to have an ambiguous attitude towards money. Objectively, it will take a certain level of money to evolve and grow – from basic eating and shelter to maybe buying a house instead of renting, buying a car, travel for pleasure, educate yourself, family and enjoy the myriad of other activities, experiences and opportunities that life offers. Some of life's enjoyable experiences are free but many are not. The theme about our relationship with money, our "money story", is developed further in Chapter 6.

When we feel sure, safe and secure with a sense of certainty, then we feel happy. However, if we have felt unsafe, unsure or threatened in the past, then our subconscious mind will have created well-worn, neural pathways that trigger uncomfortable feelings of fear and panic as it warns us to stay secure in a safe, risk-free environment. If this negative thought pattern is repeated, it can lead us to the belief that "the world is not safe" and if repeated often enough, will become an embedded neural pathway.

An example of negative behaviour in relation to QTT code 1 is a bully engaging in negative behaviour by being violent towards someone else so that they feel safe and secure. They are effectively "getting in first" to try and control the interaction and the situation. This example of a negative behaviour trying to fulfil code 1 is quite a common one.

Examples of positive behaviours that fulfil this code 1 are coming from a positive intention to be kind, enjoying quality family time and doing well at work.

In QTT, physical signs that a person is running a negative pattern around the first code SURENESS may be a physical feeling of discomfort in the pit of their stomach, equating to the First (Root/Base) Chakra.

Code 2 – DIVERSITY: Creativity, selection and risk

When code 2 is fulfilled, we feel expansive and alive, but it is much easier to fulfil this code once the basic code 1 has been fulfilled. It is not essential that we experience diversity, selection, risk and creativity, but it truly does enrich our lives over and above merely existing.

Unfortunately for a lot of people, especially in war-torn areas, where they have felt unsafe and under threat, fulfilling this code may not be so easy. Traumatic childhoods too, often result in behaviours driven by fear, overwhelm and stress and this has held people back. "Playing safe" may prevent people from moving to fulfil this code 2. Whilst not achieving the safety of code 1 they may still feel the creativity, selection and the thrill of uncertainty or risk of this second code. To achieve a totally, fulfilling life we should be looking to fulfil all seven of the QTT behavioural codes.

Gambling is a negative behaviour associated with this code. Whilst it fulfils the need for risk and excitement, it can also be financially ruinous. The same applies to the negative effects of over-eating as opposed to the positive excitement of trying out different foods. Smoking, nail-biting and drinking too much are also negative as is any destructive behaviour.

Alternatively, positive behaviours that fulfil this code can include learning new skills, a new career, travelling, finding a new partner or having a baby. These positive behaviours will challenge you, pushing you to the edge or maybe even out of your comfort zone but will enhance the creativity, risk and richness of your life.

In QTT, physical signs that a person is running a negative pattern around the second code DIVERSITY may be a physical feeling of discomfort in the mid-tummy or lower back area, equating to the Second (Sacral) Chakra.

Code 3 – IMPORTANCE: Relevance, identity, raised self-esteem

A sense of importance and self-esteem is vital for us to be happy and a lack of it can eventually lead to feelings of anxiety and even, depression.

There is a difference between a person who feels relevant and important and consequently is self-confident, self-assured and with a keen sense of self-worth (without arrogance or ego being the driver). This contrasts with a person who has a need (therefore there is a "lack") to feel important and whose behaviour is therefore based on a fear of not having it. This may result in some forms of arrogance and aggression in their behaviour.

Repeated failures experienced in the past as a child, such as academic failures, can also lead to negative thought patterns becoming embedded and knock a person's self-esteem. Bullying behaviour shown by a person trying to make someone else feel irrelevant so that they feel more important, is another example. Bullying can be done in a variety of ways. It does not necessarily have to be obviously violent or aggressive. It can be done in quite devious ways that are deliberately designed so as not to appear to be bullying. For example, by constant snide remarks designed to undermine another person's academic, financial, professional and personal achievements. It can be done in an underhand way so is not immediately obvious to others. Also, it can involve falsely accrediting a person's achievements to someone else. I have been the at the receiving end of this form of bullying and have done a lot of work understanding the mindsets involved. QTT has a very effective way of healing the underlying fall out. I needed to realise it was not my problem but the people who needed to feel secure by knocking me. The QTT Technique, "Quantum Release", enabled me to appreciate the true reality of the situation, objectively and move on from being "stuck". It also made me reframe the situations that previously triggered my discomfort.

In QTT, physical signs that a person is running a negative pattern around the third code IMPORTANCE may be a physical feeling of discomfort in their solar plexus i.e. the area at the top of your tummy just below the breast bone, equating to the Third (Solar Plexus) Chakra.

How did QTT help me – and how can it help you? See the approach to using QTT below and how it can help people.

The QTT approach is as follows:

1. Acknowledge the pattern and note where the feeling of discomfort is located when you place yourself back into the situation that is causing stress e.g. in my case, in the top of my stomach. Make sense of the feeling. The third (Solar Plexus) Chakra is the location of the discomfort and the third Behavioural Code in QTT is the aspect of my life that had been impacted upon. As I touched on previously, that in my own case, I was being deliberately misrepresented in educational, professional and personal achievements. However, now I could see the stark reality of the situation and it was totally due to the insecurities of others and their attempt to make themselves feel better by diminishing me. I used to get uncomfortable about this negative behaviour (as they purposely intended) but I now fully realised it was done out of their own insecurity to make them feel better. This is as much a form of bullying as physical aggression.

2. The next step is to release the feelings (now that I fully understood and acknowledged to myself, the nature and causes of the negative

behaviour towards me). This was done by using the Quantum Release Technique. In my case, I understood the negative behaviour of the people effectively emotionally bullying me was that they were lacking in self-esteem and that their behaviour towards me was not personal. It was an effort to make themselves feel better. The persons displaying the negative behaviour towards me had not the academic or professional qualifications, achievements and self-esteem that I possessed, and this threatened them. By understanding QTT and after a Quantum Release by Moira Geary, I learned to understand (but not condone) their negative behaviour and equally to realise that it was their problem – not mine. Under the QTT session with Moira Geary, I was finally able to release and let the feelings go and by putting their actions into an objective frame, they no longer had any relevance or influence on me. This happened in one session and was powerful. I had engaged on a previous coaching programme for several months that had not even come near to addressing the root cause of what was really causing me pain. QTT (and some NLP techniques) achieved results, quickly and I was both relieved and energised but also appreciated the help that I could potentially provide to others should I become a QTT practitioner.

3. Another example is a young girl who had failed some academic exams and eventually allowed herself to feel relevant again when she had released on her fear. The little girl was Moira Geary herself and she explains the whole scenario affecting herself in her book, "Wake up and Change your Life".

4. As referred to above, I was also able to release on the discomfort that I had felt when in receipt of negative behaviour. I now realised (both consciously but more importantly, subconsciously, where the discomfort had existed) that the bullies were acting in the only ways that they knew how to make themselves feel important. Having low self-esteem themselves, they felt better by trying to reduce my self-esteem. By reinforcing the facts of the situation and reinforcing my own realisation that their insecurities were nothing to do with me – the feeling of discomfort was gone. This release of emotion was quite remarkable and weakened the neural pathway that caused my discomfort bring triggered when on the receiving end of their negative behaviour towards me.

The release was so welcome and powerful that it made me decide that day, I would study the NLP and QTT Certification courses as these techniques genuinely do work. These techniques had helped my situation and I realised that they can certainly help others. I have seen and enabled several Quantum Releases and the relief that the individuals feel are palpable.

Regarding helping others, it is especially true regarding helping other women who face double standards and harsh criticism from society. They are expected to have careers, stay attractive yet still hold the family and domestic scene together. Women may be criticised at work if they don't work the long hours to progress their careers and then they are criticised if they are not available on the home front, for their immediate and extended families. The way society has evolved has created enormous pressure on women who work full-time whilst trying to raise families and being the main carers for ageing parents. The double guilt trip for working mothers causes a lot of unnecessary stress. This expectation and belief, that women can and should do everything, once explored and exposed for the nonsense it is, can then be shifted. Society does not judge their male colleagues as being "bad dads" if they are put in a regular working overtime situation nor are they expected to be the main carers.

I also decided to study Life Coaching and become a qualified coach in addition to certifying in NLP and QTT in 2016, to ensure that I would give the best contribution possible to help my future clients who may be struggling unnecessarily.

5. In my own case, my perception of the reality of the situation had changed. This is another very important learning. You cannot directly change other people's behaviour, but you can change your reaction to it. Clearly, there would be no point in expecting to change the other people's negative behaviour. That realisation to change their behaviour would have to come from them. However, their behaviour no longer held any significance for me and my perception of the entire situation had changed. By disassociating from toxic people who contribute nothing but only use you and are negative, is quite an effective solution to retaining your own good, positive energy and avoiding unnecessary stressful situations. I and so many others I have spoken to, have realised and understood this truth. There are people who drain your energy. Much better to choose to spend time with those who are positive and who energise you.

Other examples of negative behaviours that the subconscious believes supports the code 3 Importance behavioural code are:

- Throwing tantrums.
- Being dishonest.
- Obsessed with gaining material wealth.
- Looking for attention through destructive behaviours.
- Irresponsibly participating in dangerous sports or activities.
- Showing violence towards someone else.

Code 4 – LOVE: Self-love, giving and receiving love

This code 4 LOVE – includes three parts.
Firstly, "self-love", secondly "giving love" and finally "receiving love".

"Self-love" is an area where women particularly struggle. Society plus most religions, historically and currently, expect women to put others first and not to be seen being kind to ourselves. It is particularly important for women to realise that self-love and self-care are essential for their well-being and it is not being selfish. There are many selfish men and women who abuse others and this selfishness and greed often weakens our own self-love. This is especially true if the needs of others are constantly being placed above our own needs. Women as well as men can be narcissistic and use and manipulate people purely for their own purposes. Remember, it is easier to manipulate a person who has not developed their individual self-love. Therefore, this is another good reason to be aware of practising self-love.

The concept of self-love is changing slowly but logically it is a necessity. Basically, if we do not love ourselves and always put ourselves last, we are sending out a signal that is almost inviting others to use us and they often will. For us to have the capacity to healthily give and receive love, *we too also need to love and respect ourselves.* We should not always put ourselves last.

Positive behaviours around the second aspect to Code 4 of giving love (as opposed to the first aspect of this code of "self-love"), include:

- Helping others
- Caring for others
- Being kind

The motivation behind the actions must also be authentic as in not just doing charity work to seek approval from others or giving to get back. Genuine giving is never done to seek reward, praise or to seek acceptance.

Destructive, negative behaviours associated with this code include:

- Overeating
- Smoking
- Nail biting
- Drinking too much

All the above give short-term comfort to make us feel comfortable and loved but by then forming this to become an embedded belief (a neural pathway) equating the unhealthy habits with a quick fix to make us feel better, we experience guilt. Feeling guilt does not make us feel good in the longer term.

In the short-term, bullies can carry out violent, destructive behaviour to make themselves feel more secure, important and even to demonstrate self-love. In the long term, this behaviour will not work.

Positive behaviours associated with receiving love (the third aspect of the Behavioural Code 3 of "love") include:

- Allowing yourself to receive love from someone close to you.
- Allowing yourself to receive love from pets.
- Dropping your resistance to receiving love even if past hurts may be challenging this resolve.

In QTT, physical signs that a person is running a negative pattern around the fourth code LOVE may be a physical feeling of discomfort in your heart or chest, equating to the Fourth (Heart) Chakra.

Code 5 – AUTHENTIC VOICE: Speaking your truth, being authentic

We all know that it is important to be truthful and in expressing the truth to avoid hurting others and/or prompting a backlash. Speaking your truth can be done directly or if this is not going to serve any good purpose, can be expressed in a letter that does not need to be posted. Even by talking out loud to get something out of your system whilst for e.g. on a walk, can release on this.

Other ways of expressing authenticity include:

- The clothes you wear

- The hobbies you enjoy
- The books you read
- The friends you keep

If you feel stifled and frustrated, consider each area of your life, maybe noting in a journal the areas that you are unhappy or unfulfilled. Your subconscious is telling you that you are selling yourself short. It is worth paying attention.

It could be that when expressing an opinion – you are ignored, dismissed or told that your opinion is irrelevant or stupid. If this is repeated often enough, then you may internalise it into your own negative self-talk. The neural pathway has now been established to make you feel uncomfortable upon experiencing certain triggers. This in turn, will create a behavioural pattern to tell yourself to stay quiet. This damages self-esteem, self-expression and your confidence.

To develop upon this idea further, your subconscious may also run a pattern to deflect from the truth to stop you from being hurt. This takes the form of the ego creating a social mask. By people displaying patterns of pretending to be smarter, happier, richer and more intelligent than they are, the ego is hiding the real person behind the social mask, for protection.

Positive behaviours include enjoying the clothes, books etc. that you personally prefer.

In QTT, physical signs that a person is running a negative pattern around the fifth code AUTHENTIC VOICE may be a physical feeling of discomfort in your throat equating to the Fifth (Throat) Chakra.

Code 6 – EVOLUTION   Growth and progression

This fulfilment of this code brings much energy, joy, growth, expansion and vitality into our lives. Conditioning is very powerful. It plays a huge part in blocking our ability to progress and achieve our dreams. We may use excuses such as something is too challenging or impossible. Alternatively, we may simply give up on an idea, dream or project because we feel that we may fail or that we may be judged by others in a negative way. Usually, the real reason is that we do not evolve is not wanting to feel judged as a failure with the pain of shame and disappointment it brings. There are many excuses to self-sabotage our best intentions and to hold us back from achieving our goals.

Growth and progression will always require a challenge as we are moving out of our comfort zone to stretch ourselves and grow. Naturally, this will be uncomfortable and sometimes our desire to remain comfortable is greater than our desire to take on the new project, learn the new language or to achieve whatever growth and progression in the area we are embarking upon. It is necessary to take that leap of faith and believe in ourselves so that we stick to our plans and achieve our goals.

By progressing and growing, we can have renewed purpose and vigour in life, a sense of achievement and satisfaction. We can do this in many areas:

- Education
- Spirituality
- Personal Growth
- Careers
- Business
- Health
- Finances
- Relationships
- Hobbies

This code of Evolution is very much related to the second code of creativity, diversity, selection and risk. If we do not feel safe and secure (first code) or have trauma around the third code of self-esteem, importance, relevance and identity – then this Evolution code 6 may possibly be blocked.

Positive behaviours around growth are learning, practicing and enjoying and growing in any of the listed areas above.

In QTT, physical signs that a person is running a negative pattern around the sixth code EVOLUTION may be a physical feeling of discomfort in your head. This feeling is like frustration or overwhelm, equating to the Sixth (Eye or Cobra) Chakra.

Code 7 – CONNECTION: No separation, belonging, connecting

This code fulfils the need of belonging and being connected.
The areas of connection are:

- **Belonging with yourself** – assisted by self-love and being comfortable with yourself. This a fundamental area of connection.

- **Partnership with two people** – may be intimate, siblings or in business so that you do not feel alone. This too is a fundamental area of connection.
- **Belonging to a group** – e.g. class, college, sports team etc.
- **Belonging to larger groups** – e.g. county, country, continent, world, universe and any other groups not previously mentioned.

The idea that there is no separateness and that we all belong to a single universe (despite many automatically dismissing this concept) helps us to attain spiritual growth. Collaboration, community and contribution replace separateness, competition and comparison and ultimately leads us to achieve a sense of peace.

The fulfilment of this code cannot occur unless the other six codes are being fulfilled. Another reason that this Code 7 of Connection will not be fulfilled is that we have learned that it is not safe to connect. This belief is not necessarily true and is caused by our past conditioning and experiences.

It will be hard to achieve this spiritual connectivity level, but positive attitudes such as giving because you can and staying humble are both helpful behaviours.

In QTT, physical signs that a person is running a negative pattern around the seventh code CONNECTION may be a feeling of being disconnected equating to the Seventh (Crown) Chakra.

Chapter 3

Shifting Blocks and Negative Behaviour

Einstein and the Law of Attraction

We have already introduced Einstein's Law of Attraction and the consequent understanding that it is better to vibrate at a high frequency to attract other high frequency individuals and opportunities. This in turn, opens the prospect of making more positive connections in career, business leads and friendships with like-minded people therefore resulting in greater success personally and professionally.

Just to revise the main aspects of the Law of Attraction, below is an extract from an article in the Huffington Post by Carla Schesser.

"Everything is Vibration"

The first concept to wrap your head around is understanding the fundamental law of the Universe – the Law of Vibration.

Everything from the largest stars and planets in space, all the way down to the tiniest grain of sand, is in a constant state of vibration.

This can be difficult to believe as everything around us seems so solid. If everything is vibration, why can't I put my hand right through this computer that I'm now typing on? The answer is found within the terms frequency and arrangement.

Your brain is so smart that it has taken the vibrations all around you and learned how to translate it into your "reality" in a way so that you can't even recognise its vibration. Think about it... what are the colours that you perceive? If you've studied any science, then you know that colour is just a vibration at a specific frequency. What are the sounds that you hear? They are nothing more than vibrations that your brain has translated to make sense out of it.

From this knowledge, it can be stated that your entire "reality" is all within your head. There is nothing "out there" even though it seems like it. It's the case of the popular question: "If a tree falls in a forest and nobody's there to hear it, does it make a sound?" The idea is that you cannot experience your reality without actively perceiving it and this is the fundamental basis of the Law of Attraction.

Even after you have proof that everything around you is vibration it is still very hard for us to grasp this on an emotional level (this just emphasises how weak our logic is compared to our emotions). Logically, accepting this truth is much different than believing this truth and applying it to your life.

Stay with me, it will all start making sense.

To begin consciously creating your reality, begin believing that everything is vibration. Take some time out of your day by just sitting around and attempting to visualise the vibrational nature of everything around you. Quiet your mind and really feel the vibration of the sounds and the air around you. Suspend any doubts you may have for just a few minutes and give it a go. I think you'll be pleasantly surprised.

Like Attracts Like

The second concept to grasp is that the fundamental principle of the Law of Vibration is that vibrations of similar frequency are drawn together.

Think about two droplets of water that are slowly moving towards each other. What happens as they get closer? They eventually get close enough that they attract each other and become one droplet of water instead of two separate ones. This occurs because they are of like vibration. Now, think about the same phenomena with a droplet of water and a droplet of oil. No matter how close you put them together they will not become one with each other. This is because their vibrations are too different from one another.

This is the idea that the Law of Attraction is based on. If you want to bring about something in your life, regardless of what it is, begin vibrating at a level that is congruent with your desired reality.

This is such a huge idea!

Think about it!

If 1) Everything is vibration and, 2) Vibrations of similar frequencies are drawn together and, 3) You possess the ability to control your vibration; then you can most certainly control the conditions of your life!

The problem comes about whenever we attempt to control our reality without first adjusting our vibration. No amount of physical manipulation will create the world that we wish to see. All the work is done on the inside, in our minds. This means that no amount of action alone will produce the results that we desire. However, once we gain the ability to condition our minds to our desired frequencies of vibration, our physical reality quickly follows suit and reflects our new vibration.

Take the time to think deeply about these ideas and see if they don't make sense to you both logically and emotionally. If you think long and hard enough you will come to the same conclusions that the great leaders of humanity's past have all come to: that is, "we create our own reality".

I believe that the above article is very insightful and explains the Law of Attraction in a very straightforward way, especially the far-reaching effects witnessed by increasing the frequency of your vibration.

Law of Attraction and Self-Limiting Beliefs

Following on from this article and appreciating the Law of Attraction, we can also understand that if we hold self-limiting, negative beliefs, then these can unwittingly hold us back from achieving our objectives and reaching our full potential.

By examining our values and beliefs, looking at our dreams and aspirations using a vision board and journal, we have identified what we genuinely want. We can translate some of those visions into goals and we can also identify the negative behaviours that we need to shift to allow us to achieve those goals. With the negative beliefs shifted and replaced with positive beliefs, we are ready to vibrate at higher frequencies and attract what we want, making our dreams and goals, a reality.

Before outlining the techniques that can be used to shift negative beliefs, there is some more explanation required to clarify to the logical, conscious mind, so that it really understands what is happening. By doing this the subconscious mind will become realigned to the conscious mind and progress can occur unhindered. NLP and QTT can help us to do this.

Neuro Linguistic Programming (NLP)

NLP is an approach to self-improvement and self-management using a set of rules and techniques proposed for modifying behaviour and producing more effective communication. This is one route to shifting blocks and negative behaviour.

NLP itself, is an acronym for:

(N) = Neuro i.e. the Neuro aspect relates to the nervous system through which we receive our experiences via our five senses and how we process them internally.

(L) = Linguistic i.e. the Linguistic aspect relates to language and non-verbal communication systems through which our internal view of the world, known as "Internal Representational Systems" are coded, written, ordered and given meaning.

(P) = Programming i.e. this relates to the person's ability to run patterns, programmes and strategies to achieve a desired outcome.

NLP was developed in the 1970s by John Grinder (a US Management Consultant) and Richard Bandler (a US Psychologist), who studied selected leaders in their fields by modelling their language and behaviour patterns using the Neuro, Linguistic and Programming aspects above.

The diagram below summarises the theory behind NLP:

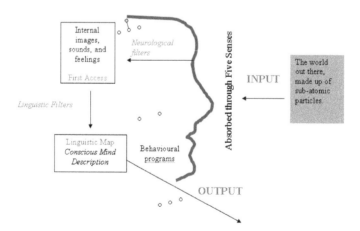

I learned this modality of NLP (and the QTT modality) through Moira Geary who has collated the wisdom of NLP and QTT in the "Golden Rules" below. Whilst QTT draws on some of the learnings from NLP, it fast tracks the results. Everyone wants relief from what has been causing pain, holding us back and the quicker the results are achieved, the better.

Many of the "talking therapies" dealt with later in the book are very useful too but these can also take a long time to achieve results.

Understanding the basic Assumptions of NLP and QTT – The Golden Rules

1. **"Respect how others see their model of the world."**

   Individuals form their own unique "model" of the world as they journey through life.

   This is especially so, in their formative years from 0–8 years old (as defined by UNESCO), when the initial memories and feelings of various experiences and beliefs are first formed. There is a variety of influences that colour an individual's perception of the world both in the formative years and later years. The main influencers on our unique model of the world include parents or guardians, family, teachers, peers, society, culture, country and religion, which together with the individual's own innate personalities (and genetic predisposition) all come together to impact on a person's understanding of the world. The perceived reality or model of the world that is formed can be rewritten and changed as we continue throughout our journey. The ability to change our perceived reality or model of the world is an important one and should give everyone hope.

   It is essential to fully understand that the behaviour a person displays, even if very negative and destructive e.g. arrogant, aggressive, ignorant or deceitful is a result of the factors described above. Whilst not agreeing or condoning negative and destructive behaviour, at least we can go some way to understanding it. The NLP school of thought also adds the neurological filters into the mix of factors that influence our perception or model of the world. (The neurological filters include our brains generalising, distorting or deleting certain pieces of information received by it via the five senses of touch, sight, feeling, hearing or taste).

   The memories and feelings associated with our experiences are stored away in our subconscious minds. Our resulting behaviour is based on our unique experiences, values and beliefs as impacted by the neurological filters.

2. **"In being respectful of everyone's model of the world, do not be judgmental."**

As mentioned previously, negative behaviour that results from a person's specific model of the world (that does not have to be the same as our model) can be changed. If that behaviour is not serving a person, it is possible by careful questioning to identify the root causes of the beliefs producing that behaviour. Then to shift the perception to become a more positive one. An example could be that once a bully (who has bullied in a physical or emotional way) understands their behaviour, it may happen that the bullying behaviour stops. Alternatively, if there is narcissism involved or mental health issues, this may not be the case.

Adopting a non-judgmental approach is very useful, especially as we tend in the first instance to be the most critical of ourselves. Second on the list of people that we are critical of, are the people we love most. Finally, we then criticize family and friends.

If we can drop the shame, guilt, fear and anger (the feelings that vibrate at the lowest frequencies), it is so much easier to make progress. Comparing ourselves with others to prove we are better or are always right, may feed our ego but it is unnecessary, unhelpful and disturbs our inner peace.

No baby was born with the intention of hurting others and it is important to keep that at the forefront of our minds.

3. **"The ability to change our perspective and experience of our reality is often more valuable than trying to change our reality."**

Sometimes we should reframe the circumstances so that we get an unfamiliar perspective on a situation. We can always change our perspective and it is a lot easier and less frustrating than trying to change the world or other people's perspective. Instead, we can explore deeper and understand where the behaviour is coming from. Following on from this, we can change our own reaction to it and maybe not get upset when someone is short with us. Rather than viewing the situation from our model of the world, step back and appreciate that there are usually many different interpretations of a situation.

Perhaps there are other larger concerns within the life of the person who is abrupt with us that we do not know about or even do not understand. If we were in possession of all the facts and understood the total situation fully, then we would realise that the shortness was not actually personally directed towards us. We may be irrelevant in the whole scheme of things. By changing our future perception, we will not automatically react by being upset but will have the wisdom to appreciate that all may not be as it seems.

During the most recent economic recession in Ireland, people could buy into the general gloomy and negative attitude and decide not to setup a new business. Alternatively, they could decide to change this perception. They could realise, on a more positive note, that there may be new opportunities and appreciate that changed events allow us the scope to move on, explore and maybe offer services to help people in an alternative way. The reality has not changed (the recession continued), however, the perception towards it has changed. Opportunity, rather than negativity, was the new attitude and it works.

4. "All behaviour has a positive intention."

This is true because the subconscious is always trying to protect us – even if the patterns of behaviour we exhibit because of embedded beliefs are negative or even dangerous. The bully's subconscious mind has learnt that getting in first and behaving aggressively is the best way to scare off the perceived threat and protect themselves from others. Their protective mechanism is to frighten the other threat away or to intimidate them as they are perceived to be a danger to them. The perceived threat is usually not a real threat.

This perception may not be a correct or helpful one for a bully in viewing their own situation but perhaps the bully has learned this protective response because they themselves had been bullied throughout their own childhood. They learned that this behaviour is the way to deal with perceived or real threats. So that is what they do.

Again, it does not justify the negative behaviour but allows it to be understood and once appreciated by the bully, it can then be shifted.

You can only allow change if you are aware of what you need to change. The subconscious will always try to protect us emotionally and physically so that we may be truly happy. Both the conscious and subconscious minds must be fully aligned for inner peace and progression in life. Once the conscious mind can start to make sense of the negative behaviour i.e. that the subconscious mind of the bully believes that acting this way will protect the bully, then practical alternative solutions and behaviours can be considered.

5. **"Resources exist within each one of us to be able to be happy, caring, strong and to change."**

We appreciate that when we were born, that our unconditioned, subconscious mind was a blank canvas. The absence of any "blocks" can be clearly demonstrated if we observe the natural confidence, energy, vigorous work and creativity of children. They have not yet had negative experiences in most cases. If we look within ourselves now as adults, we can rediscover these attributes and unblock the anger, worry and irritation that block the positivity that we naturally possess. The confidence, energy, ability to work hard and be creative are all attributes that still exist within us. Sometimes they just need to be unlocked once again. We can be creative, fearless, confident, loving and open to learning and to experience without fear, as we once were, as children.

Fear and Disempowering Fear

There is a compelling school of thought, stating that the two most powerful emotions are love and fear. If we are in a state of fear, then we block manifestation. It is important to remember that fear is just our subconscious mind trying to protect us, even if the fear is misplaced. An example of this is the fear of speaking in public.

However, if we dig deeper, it is not actually the fear of public speaking itself – it is the fear of rejection and that we will be laughed at or maybe we are not good enough. Our fear is based around how we will cope if that happens.

We all have the resources within us to overcome our fears as we know we were born with these resources. That is why young children are so uninhibited and authentically enjoy the trivial things. Remember the confident little child who got up to sing happily from their heart? They can still sing but their subconscious is trying to protect them from the fear of rejection and if they are told to be quiet, they will. They can still sing perfectly well much in the same way that all of us are well able to speak in public, did we not have a negative self-belief limiting us.

I have an association with both lack of confidence in singing and playing the piano. Both of which I know I am addressing. The piano experience arose from being stopped practising the piano at home, which in turn meant that I wasn't as prepared for my lessons as I (and my piano teacher) would have liked me to have been. I was disturbing my brother from his studies. Hilarious, especially for anyone who knows how studious my brother was! I have my own piano now (something I vowed I would do one day) so I can practise away whenever I want.

The block about singing comes from an incident when I was at boarding school, and just turned twelve. (I was only in boarding school in Ireland that one year as my family lived in England. Long story!). I was happily singing and playing a song when an older girl came into the room and scolded me saying that the song was one of the songs chosen for an upcoming surprise concert. I replied that how would there be any link made, as I was playing many songs not included in the concert. I got dropped from that concert the very next day. To be honest, it hurt and put me off music for quite some time, and it wasn't long after that when I was back in England that our piano disappeared. My mother had given it away as no one used it. The logic of it all!

We must examine why we think that we cannot do something and see when exactly we decided to put the meaning on the experience and then disempower that belief. Remember that beliefs are not facts.

Most fears are based on beliefs from our life experiences and the associated negative memories. We need to release the fears so that we can live life to our full potential. Quantum Release techniques do just this.

Basic Quantum Release Technique – QTT

This QTT technique has been developed by Moira Geary.

After years of studying and practicing several modalities including NLP, hypnosis, timeline etc. Moira began to amalgamate all her knowledge and experience to enable her clients to get emotional relief from their pain. This Basic Quantum Release technique releases negative, embedded thought patterns and removes the "stuck" emotions associated with them.

If we release negative thoughts which also store feelings and memories associated with them (in our subconscious), then we are allowing more space for positive feelings. We have a better chance to manifest positively and vibrate and attract at a higher energy level when we possess more positive feelings.

If there is an object in your home that holds bad memories and associations causing you to feel a negative sensation in the pit of your stomach, then using the Basic Quantum Release technique can release both the memory and associated emotions around that object.

A skilled and qualified QTT practitioner will be able to drill down with more powerful questions to get to the source of this discomfort and then enable a release of both associated feelings and memories surrounding the object. You really do need to "feel" the process, not just skip through it lightly. Clearly, releasing around objects is only a starting point to the use of this technique and it can be used on deeper, more embedded and complex issues and thought patterns.

Advanced Quantum Release Technique - QTT

This technique has again been developed by Moira Geary – and is a powerful technique that should be done with a qualified QTT practitioner. It is far more complex than the Basic Quantum Release and consequently, should be used in more complex situations to release trauma.

"The ecology of outcomes must be evaluated before change is instigated."

In the example of bullying, it is more than likely "ecologically good" (or will produce an acceptable outcome) to shift the bullying behaviour. In some instances, there may however, be other repercussions that follow on from such shifts that may cause even further problems once the original behaviour has changed. The potential fallout should always be considered. This is exactly why the skilled questioning, communication and understanding of the entire scenario must be diligently and empathetically carried out by the QTT Practitioner prior to attempting any shift. The entire situation and ramifications of any important change must be evaluated carefully before any change is made. Sometimes effecting change may not be the optimal solution and the knock-on results may not be useful.

I have witnessed Advanced Quantum Release Technique working in a variety of situations regarding a whole array of issues – from early childhood traumas to family, work, new businesses and relationship situations. Once the emotional block is removed and the emotions around it are released, progress can then be made in a much lighter, uninhibited and positive frame of mind.

Stepping out of your Comfort Zone

Most of us are afraid of moving outside of our comfort zones, so we obviously remain stuck and are therefore unable to progress to achieve the goals we consciously desire.

One way to overcome this is to imagine our comfort zone as a circle, as in the diagram below. If we step outside the comfort zone, we do not need to imagine stepping into eternity as that is too scary; instead, imagine another bigger circle around the smaller one. This can be used again when we have decided to take another "leap into the unknown", so we step into the next outer circle and so on. This method allows us to reassure ourselves that we are still progressing, in a gradual, controlled way and are not going completely into outer space. By controlling the pace of change we are less likely to become overwhelmed.

We can use this increasing circle concept to envisage the safety of moving on to the next stage in our life and conquering the next comfort zone.

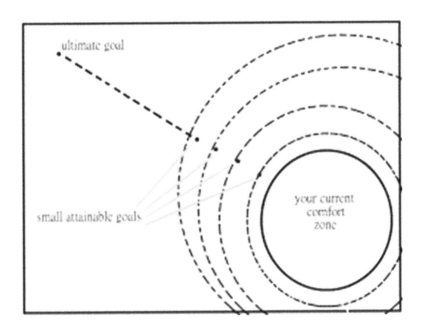

EXERCISE:

Examine your own situation. Is there something that you would dearly love to do but it seems unreachable? It may not be so unreachable after all. Jot down your ideas, thoughts, hopes and fears as they occur to you instinctively.

Examine what you have written down.

What are the benefits and how will you feel if you do achieve this goal?

Do a first draft of your step-by-step plan to achieve the goal. The plan can always be refined. Consider if you need any resources such as attending further training or coaching and factor this into your first draft plan if it applies.

Now look at your fears. Can you overcome your fears if you adopt the approach above, regarding stepping out of your comfort zone in a staged manner?

Can you see how the goal is now reachable - if you approach it in this way?

Set yourself timelines for the different steps in the plan and just do it!

Procrastination and how to deal with it

Everyone at one time or another is guilty of procrastination. To overcome procrastination, it helps to understand it. Procrastination occurs whenever we make excuses or allow ourselves to become distracted, despite feeling that we want to do something. We need to realise that something inside of us is stopping us from doing the very thing that we want to do.

The reason for procrastination usually lies within us, in our subconscious, so we need to work it out on a conscious level first, so that we can correct it. Then both conscious and subconscious minds will be aligned. Procrastination can happen in any area of our life be it work, sales, business, fitness, relationships, health or even spiritual goals.

We have set our goals and we have devised a plan, so we know the necessary steps we must take to achieve them. We need motivation and that usually stems from focusing on the benefits of the desired outcomes that our goals will help us achieve, as opposed to concentrating on the process that we must engage in to get there. Getting fit is a challenge, being fit is a joy. It brings physical, mental, emotional and energetic rewards. The first steps are always the most difficult. I love plants, flowers and trees and so enjoy my garden. The thoughts of weeding, however, do not appeal to me one bit. Nevertheless, to motivate myself to begin the weeding process, I imagine the pleasurable outcome rather than dwelling on the routine process of weeding. The beautiful plants, herbs, fruits and flowers that will be allowed to grow and thrive once the weeds have been removed are my motivation. It is very useful therefore to focus on the desired end-result rather than the painful process of getting there.

How do we overcome procrastination?

Focus on the outcome of enjoying the smells, appearance and the energy of a beautiful garden attracting insects, birds and wildlife, dogs, cats and people. Enjoying it, instead of focusing on the more mundane task of weeding is a good strategy.

Overcoming procrastination will take effort but use **the motivation of concentrating on how we will feel when we achieve the goal and get results**. After a while, the weeding routine will become easier, especially when you start feeling and seeing the progress being made. The same is true of becoming physically fitter. As we become fitter, our energy level increases as does our vibration. A higher vibration will attract other opportunities into our lives at every level. Physical fitness improves mental and emotional fitness, makes us happier and problem solving is easier. It's a no-brainer really. So, appreciating how we will feel when we achieve the goal is another way to tackle procrastination.

Fear of stepping out of our comfort zone may also be another reason for procrastination. So, we can use the **"Stepping out of your Comfort Zone" model.** We experience fear on several levels when we do step out. For example, we may be fearful of other people's opinions regarding subjects as diverse as our choice of garden plants or going to the gym. We may not want to stand out too much from our neighbours' style of garden in case we fail or attract criticism. It may be easier to play safe. We may avoid the gym because we do not want other gym users to judge how unfit we are and how we look. Additionally, we may worry that we will fail to get fit even after suffering all this discomfort.

We could have fears that the plants in our garden or in our house won't grow, especially if we have been adventurous in our choice of plants. I embarked upon a commercial organic strawberry project which attracted shed loads of naysayers all telling me how I wouldn't succeed but I did!

All the self-doubts can begin to plague us so that we may just not bother with all the weeding or attempting to grow different plants. An easy and understandable option but is not necessarily the best, in the long-term. **Visualising** the satisfaction and joy we will **feel** once we have a beautiful garden with delicious, healthy organic strawberries to enjoy is a useful approach.

We can use the "Stepping out of your Comfort Zone" model in the gardening and getting fit examples, as follows. If we imagine our current comfort zone as a circle (as in the diagram in the previous section) within which we are comfortable such as being relatively unfit or having a neglected and slightly overgrown garden. Then try to imagine that there is an even larger circle outside of that one and that is where we will be stepping into. It could be a short daily walk to start with if we are thinking of getting fit. It could be mowing the lawn. In thinking this way, we are containing the space into which we are stepping out and then it is more achievable. Stepping out into an infinite, unknown and scary space is a daunting thought. Use a step-by-step approach and slowly build up to a more rigorous workout rather than attempting these at the outset of your exercise programme. Tackle weeding different areas of the garden then planting colourful plants and flowers. You will also feel energised and grow your confidence and self-esteem when you do manage to achieve these mini-milestones and gradually expand your horizons. As you navigate and achieve one goal, you can then have others and step into even bigger circles and milestones on your journey. Eventually, you will achieve your goal of fitness and/or having a beautiful garden.

It will help stop procrastination if you believe that the outcome is compelling enough to achieve. If you are only half-heartedly looking to plan your garden or to lose a few pounds, then your motivation will also be half-hearted. You will not increase your energy vibration levels unless your outcome is compelling enough. If you are doing it to please others – then this will also not work – it must be done for yourself. You need a burning desire to do this. Getting your head in the right place so that your *conscious and subconscious are aligned* is much more likely to achieve a successful, longer-term result. You also need to place a higher value on designing and nurturing that garden or getting fit rather than on the comfort of not weeding or exercising.

Focus on your contribution (linked to the above about how compelling your goal is). **Code 7 of QTT is to contribute at a spiritual level**. When you achieve your fitness goal, you will not only be fitter, healthier but also happier and more confident in your abilities. You are in a better place, feeling more energetic and vibrating at a higher frequency. You will then be of more value to yourself, your family and your customers or clients. Indeed, you will be in a better space to contribute to your wider community. In this way, there is a positive ripple effect that goes from you out to the wider community. Increasing the frequency of your vibration will also attract abundant manifestation.

Internal Saboteur (negative self-talk), Solutions and "Mini-miens".

The negative self-talk mentioned above in the section about the nature of "Procrastination" is our subconscious trying to protect us from feeling let down, ashamed and being hurt. Whilst the intention is always good i.e. trying to protect us, we all appreciate at some level that it is beneficial to stretch and challenge ourselves, grow, develop, learn and progress out of our comfort zones rather than stagnating in a safe, non-challenging cocoon and not experiencing life to the full.

In QTT, various aspects of our personalities are referred to as "mini-miens". The Oxford English dictionary defines a "mien" as "a person's appearance or manner, especially as an indication of their character or mood". It is good to be aware that we all have many distinct aspects to our personalities and we move into them naturally. Some are good, such as "Motivator", "Warrior", "Entertainer", whilst others are not so good. Everyone knows people who love to slip into "Victim Mode", but it does not serve anyone to always be in a victim mode, despite the attention it may initially gain. By continually playing the victim, a person will stay stuck in that mode and use it as an excuse not to learn, grow or develop.

The mini-miens help us, as they are all facets of our personalities that we employ as needed. Little children easily slip in and out of them, especially when playing "Super Hero!" It is a tonic to observe little children playing. One of my favourite TV programmes is "The Secret Lives of Five-Year-olds". It is a joy to watch and is so insightful, funny, heart-warming and heart-breaking watching them tackle their feelings and challenge their preconceptions as they grow and learn how to experience living a happy life.

The mini-mien at work in the example of getting fit but procrastinating about taking the necessary action to do this, may be the "Doubter" mini-mien. To remain reliant on the "Doubter" can become very destructive as you will not progress out of your comfort zone due to fear. As a result, you will remain in a behavioural pattern that will not allow development, growth or progression. Sacrificing development, growth and progression all for the sake of staying "comfortable" is not a beneficial trade-off. The "Doubter" is in effect an internal saboteur and to grow personally and professionally we need to take the energy out of it and dissolve the strength of the saboteur.

The internal saboteur is the subconscious internal voice telling you to "stay in bed and feel more comfortable", "eat more cake; it will make you feel better", "have another glass of wine and it will relax you". Whilst this is meant to make us feel better, it is only a short-term fleeting comforting feeling that our conscious mind knows is not the best, long-term choice.

That is the internal conflict that is going on and this can last for years, leaving people "stuck" and unable to achieve their goals. Again, if this negative self-talk happens enough times, the belief will then become embedded and will cause people to stop moving forward to achieve any goals or dreams. "You are too old". "Who are you to do that?" "You don't have the ability!" And so on...

It is best to acknowledge and be grateful for the role of protection that the subconscious provides when it raises a red flag to warn us of the possibility of failure or other uncomfortable emotions. However, we can objectively look at the dialogue and see if it is logical or purely coming from a place of fear and unnecessarily holding us back.

Sometimes we can disempower the internal saboteur by interrupting the negative neural pathways that the saboteur has caused to be set up or by using the NLP "Parts Integration" Technique discussed in the next section. In other cases, there may be further complications and additional techniques other than just "Parts Integration" involved. Yet again, there may be another more suitable technique than "Parts Integration" to disempower the internal saboteur.

EXERCISE:

Examine each area of your life and note anything that is going on at an internal saboteur level causing you to be "stuck" or holding you back from pursuing some of your goals or dreams. List them all down. Then the following techniques can be used to break or interrupt the embedded neurological pattern so that you can move on and "unstick" yourself. The assistance of a coach may be beneficial in this situation as they can objectively question and drilldown into what is really going on.

Pattern Interrupt Techniques

This essentially refers to techniques to interrupt embedded neural linguistic pathways running automatic programmes in our brain. It is important to understand what a neural linguistic pathway is before we attempt to interrupt it. A neural linguistic pathway is a bundle of myelin-covered neurons (the white matter in the brain). They provide a connection between one part of the nervous system and another.

Whenever we learn something, a new neural pathway is created in the brain. The more we use those neural pathways over the years, they become deeply embedded into deeper portions of the brain. This is the case when we form habits. The more we perform the habit, then the more embedded it becomes. Equally, the less that pathway is used then the weaker the pathway and the habit becomes.

A "Pattern Interrupt" is when a series of deliberate interruptions are performed and break an existing neurological link, (also known as an "embedded neuro-linguistic pathway" in NLP). This could be done to break a habit or to change a state (or way a person is feeling).

On a very simple level, it can be used to "Pattern Interrupt" a crying child by pointing out to the child that there is a dog running around. This distracts the child and interrupts and stops their crying behaviour as they become more interested in the dog. Their automatic programme has been broken as they maybe for example crying for attention but have now switched their focus to the dog.

There are many ways that you can pattern interrupt – by going for a walk, taking a yoga class, initiating a hand-shake, responding in an unexpected way to a person who previously always had certain expectations of the way a conversation will go or even taking time out to travel.

The "anchoring" technique (described below) and "belief change" techniques (such as using daily affirmations in Chapter 4) are even more examples of how to pattern-interrupt.

Anchoring as a Pattern Interrupt Technique

What is an Anchor?

An "Anchor" is "a stimulus which triggers a specific physiological or emotional state. It allows us to interrupt our current thought pattern by being able to access a desired, positive state, immediately. If you are thinking negative thoughts that make you feel sad, you still retain the power to control and change your way of thinking. You do not have to feel that way. I am not talking about clinical depression here, but we can all be in a depressed state as opposed to being depressed, when life events naturally bring us down.

EXERCISE – Creating your own anchor

- Choose a desired state you would like to experience as opposed to feeling in an unwanted state e.g. under stress. The desired state could be joy, peace, excitement, control or happiness.

- Recall a previous situation in your life where a certain memory evokes a feeling such as happiness or excitement. I will give you my own example as an aid to explain it, however, feel free to use your own memories to recreate whatever feelings you want to. My memory was as a young sixteen-year-old girl on holidays with my family on my uncle's farm in Ireland. The sun was shining in a blue sky with beautiful, white, fluffy cumulus clouds moving across it. I had just washed my hair and I remember the distinct, pleasant smell of Sunsilk shampoo, along with the sweet smell of fresh hay from the adjoining field. I felt on top of the world. I was lying in the grass in my uncle's meadow, completely at one with nature and not a soul in sight. I was going to a carnival later that evening. (They were called carnivals, but they were really marquees where country and western bands played and where mainly younger people danced to the music). I felt happy, excited, alive and full of energy and excitement. My hair was clean and shiny, and I had a date! Delighted with the world, I was so happy, I burst into song!

  Use all your senses to conjure up an image i.e. sight, smell, touch, sound and even taste. You must *associate* into the image i.e. you are in the scene and experiencing it by looking out through your eyes. This viewpoint is the opposite of you looking in at the scene and looking at yourself in it (i.e. disassociated).

- Also, imagine your scene as a vivid, colour film with sounds and clearly defined, moving images as this will increase the intensity of the image (as opposed to a small, silent, black and white, non-moving picture).

- When you remember your chosen image, vividly, as outlined above, recall your desired memory and feelings, then associate yourself into that image. By "associating" into the scene, you will be physically part of that memory as if it were happening now. Really concentrate internally to focus deeply and notice how you feel in your body and where you feel it.

As portrayed in the next diagram, keep thinking of that desired feeling and increase the intensity of the colour, the potency of the different senses of sight, hearing, smell, touch. Increase the speed of the moving, colourful film that you are imagining. In this way, colour, movement, speed, sound, sights, smells and even touch all become intensified in the scene that you are associated into. Then at the height of the intensity, lock the memory in for example, by squeezing the middle finger to the thumb. Repeat this practice (maybe even twenty times within a twenty-four-hour period) until you can eventually trigger the anchor and conjure up the desirable feelings, just by squeezing the middle finger and thumb when you feel your spirits need uplifting.

- In the anchoring diagram, you can see that you keep locking in the "trigger" (squeezing middle finger and thumb together) at the height of the intensity of the desired feeling.

- In this way, if you are needing to interrupt a sad feeling, and break an embedded neural pathway, you can use this trigger to shift your memory, thoughts, and feelings to one of joy in an instant once you have anchored. This is a hugely useful tool to possess.

What are the five keys to successful anchoring?

In this ITURN Model of anchoring, the five keys to successful anchoring, which can be described by acronym **ITURN**, are:

- The Intensity of the experience you are hoping to anchor.
- The Timing of the anchor. It is important to do this when the feeling is most intense.
- The Uniqueness of the anchor.
- The Replication of the stimulus.
- The Number of times that this exercise is repeated.

A diagram showing the "ITURN Model of the Anchoring Process" is shown on the following page.

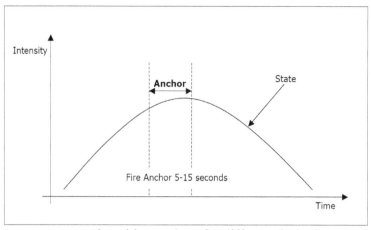

You can create several positive anchors for different desired states. A state of confidence, positivity and high energy can be anchored in to be triggered off just before a presentation, business meeting or even an exam. I used this technique and this example just before a recent Spanish oral exam to interrupt a negative belief pattern that I was not really any good at speaking Spanish. It works! That specific embedded neural linguistic pathway is now gone for good. It did hold me back from practising speaking Spanish however for fear of being ridiculed; yet, the only way to improve speaking Spanish, unsurprisingly enough, is to speak Spanish. That negative self-belief was clearly not serving me and thankfully the embedded neural linguistic pathway has been interrupted, its power has been dissipated and it no longer holds me back from practising and even enjoying speaking Spanish, without fear.

Parts Integration Technique

1. What is Parts Integration

"Parts Integration" is one of the most effective and useful NLP techniques in my experience.

It is used when distinct parts of your mind are conflicting with each other and you want to realign them. For example, one part (the conscious mind) really wants you to do something yet the other part (the sub-conscious mind) is holding you back, making you feel it is a bad move. Again, this is the subconscious trying to be protective of you. However, it is driven by the emotion of fear causing you to self-doubt and cautioning you *not* to do something. It is also the reason why despite our determination to break a bad habit, we seem to easily fall back into the old pattern, without understanding why.

When an inner conflict situation arises, it is useful to dig deeper into yourself (or a coach can do this in a more objective way) by asking: "How exactly is that a problem for you?" This will allow you to get to the crux of the dilemma. "Parts Integration" is a technique to reconcile both conflicting parts of your brain i.e. the fearful subconscious that craves security versus the logical conscious that is reaching out for freedom, action and growth. When both parts are reconciled so that they both get to understand each other and are then aligned, there will be no inner conflict and the best course of action for you to follow will become much clearer.

If the inner conflict is not resolved, then even if you have struggled to overcome the desire to e.g. comfort eat, to watch television instead of exercising or staying in an unfulfilling job rather than starting up your own business, then you will still be full of suppressed, conflicted emotions and unmet desires. Basically, you will still suffer from lack of inner alignment and this NLP technique is the solution to that dilemma.

When both the parts that are in conflict are eventually reconciled and are in alignment, then the inner conflict has been resolved and you can move forward confidently with your decision. Now that there is alignment, then there is no conflict, anxiety or indecision. This technique can be used in several situations, such as where logic conflicts with emotion, rational thinking conflicts with intuitive thinking, childhood beliefs conflict with adult beliefs.

Some specific, practical examples of inner conflict regularly experienced in our lives include:

- Starting your own business (versus staying in an unfulfilling job).
- Eating a healthy diet (versus comfort eating).
- Exercising regularly (or not!)

All of these are explored and explained further below:

Example 1 – Starting your own Business

Part of you (the logical mind) wants to leave your job and start your own business but the protective subconscious is telling you to stay in your job and enjoy the security. It is warning you about all the dangers and pitfalls of being self-employed versus being an employee. Possible fears exist around lack of financial security, fear of failure and embarrassment around what other people might think to name a few examples. However, as I show later in the case study, the other conscious mind acknowledges that there can also be huge advantages. There is an internal conflict between the two parts in your mind therefore.

Example 2 – Eating healthily versus Comfort Eating

Inner conflict can occur around eating cake (it could also be any junk food, chocolate or whatever!) or making a healthy choice in your food selection. The logical part of you wants to lose weight, look better, have more energy and be healthier whilst the subconscious mind wants you to feel comfortable and enjoy the delicious taste of cake, chocolate or whatever your weakness is.

Example 3 – Regular Exercise Routine

Exercise is another prime example of inner conflict. The logical mind wants you to become healthier by exercising regularly whilst the subconscious mind wants you to feel secure and safe and enjoy relaxing maybe in front of the television in the warmth of your living room or in your bed (depending at what time you are planning to exercise!)

In summary, the Parts Integration technique works at the subconscious level rather than at the conscious, logical level. The reason being that the logical mind is already on board as opposed to the fearful, protective, subconscious mind. This being the case, there will be a need for some imagination and at first, the technique may appear to be slightly "out there". If you can suspend your disbelief (it is better to go to a coach to experience this technique I believe) then I can personally vouch that it does emphatically work. It has worked on me and on others, particularly one client who was totally resistant to coaching in general. He was particularly sceptical of this technique even when I explained the process and the underlying reasoning behind it to him !

To explain and illustrate this NLP technique further, I have outlined a Parts Integration Process that worked successfully with this specific, sceptical client, below:

CASE STUDY:

My client was literally in two minds about embarking upon a large construction groundwork project (the subconscious saying "no", favouring security, avoiding any fear of failure – in fact, all the of the fearful aspects that I mentioned above). Alternatively, the conscious mind understood the benefits of freedom, both from a work and financial point of view and wanted to go for it. The crux of the issue was regarding setting up a company and going into business on a much larger scale involving taking more risk. The promise of potentially much greater income, more control and ultimately a greater sense of achievement and personal growth were the positives. Taking on staff and planning capital expenditure were just some of the steps outside of his comfort zone. A guaranteed, steady but lesser income and less control had been the safe, comfort zone he was used to and had never really thought of stepping outside of.

He eventually identified the true nature of the conflict and understood the two conflicting parts involved. It was basically a list of pros and cons regarding a decision that he was thinking over. After careful, probing questioning, we extracted the real information and importantly the real fears.

The client sat in a position where he could hold his arms straight out in front of him, comfortably apart from each other. He had the space to allow that they could freely come together. Each arm was also a symbolic, visual representation of the different, conflicting parts of his mind.

The part that represented the unwanted, fearful state or behaviour, came out metaphorically speaking, on to one of my client's hands. This was important because it was symbolic that it was placed outside of his body and he had disassociated from it. This left him with more space to examine that viewpoint more objectively and in a less emotional context. By carefully questioning the client and getting him to give the part specific characteristics, it was easier for him to more effectively visualise the mindset. Assigning characteristics such as imagining what it looked, sounded and felt like made the visualisation more intense. In that way he got a visual, auditory and kinaesthetic image of that part.

It is important that the client now associated into the perceptual position of this part so that he could feel and understand its true nature.

We then dealt with the part that is on the other side of the conflict. We elicited the "opposite number", the desired state, to come out on to the other hand. It can also be very practical – as my client compared the two parts as a brick (this representing the subconscious state where it is safer to stay in his current situation) versus a gold bar (the opposite number or desired state of starting up a business).

I ensured that the client had a clear visual, auditory and kinaesthetic image of both parts e.g. what does it look like, feel like, does it weigh much etc. Clearly the bright, smooth, shiny, attractive gold bar – representing this conscious part is very different to the rough, dull, clumsy looking brick of the previous, subconscious part. The client focused deeply on this desired part and associated into the new, shiny perceptual position.

We then asked both parts, would they be willing to work together to help each other achieve their highest positive intention for the client. We asked if they realised that they are both part of a larger whole, that of the mind. This reasoning is necessary to align both states of mind.

The hands eventually started to move together as the two parts began to realise that they were part of a larger whole and that they had the same intention.

We separated the intention from the behaviour i.e. we chunked up to see an overview of both parts.

Both parts were reframed i.e. both sides to the argument, so that they realised that they had the same intention. The intention was to allow growth but in a protected way. This is then summarised by chunking up to see the overall picture and reinforce the learning. Questioning occurred regarding: What was the positive intention of this part? What was the purpose? Why did it want to do that in a positive way? We moved from one hand to the other asking questions until we got both parts to "see" the common ground. This technique helped the client's brain to rationalise what was happening. There was an exchange going on between the two parts so that they moved towards a common goal with no fear or mistrust of the opposite part.

It was necessary to repeat this process several times until both parts came to agree on a higher intention which was the positives of running his own business from a financial and personal viewpoint. The risks were also addressed, and the subconscious part was now reassured. Each part communicated with the other and noticed what resources or features were needed for the other part to be reassured.

When the hands did not immediately come together automatically, I made appropriate suggestions to help the process. Eventually, the client realised that both parts of his brain had the same intention. They were both part of the greater whole and they wanted to connect. When this connection was successfully made, the hands moved together, slowly.

Once the hands joined, then there was a true integration and a mutual understanding by both the conscious and the subconscious. The merged parts were taken back inside the body and they merged back into the wholeness inside. By the hands being allowed to come together they then brought the new integrated parts into his heart. This was done symbolically when the joined hands physically touched his heart area.

I then asked him how he felt and if the inner conflict was gone. This was tested by asking how he felt when he associated himself back into a situation that previously caused him the inner conflict regarding setting up his own business. As there was now no inner conflict, the block had gone so the parts integration had been successful. Then I tested, the effectiveness of the "Parts Integration" technique, using a tool called "future pacing". This involved getting the client to imagine how he would feel about the previously held conflicting views in the future. For example, how he thought he would feel in the situation (that previously caused him conflict) in one day, one week, one month, one year etc. from that point in time. This "future pacing" was done immediately after the "Parts Integration" had occurred. The Parts Integration technique was effective because in all the future paced situations, the client felt no conflict as the parts were fully integrated.

This technique should be done by a qualified NLP or QTT Practitioner as it is very important to explain all aspects of the process being performed.

In the above "Parts Integration" Technique – a brick symbolised the more negative attitude of staying put in a relatively secure, steady and safe place with no danger of failing. On the other hand (quite literally!), a gold bar symbolised the more positive approach of stretching the client, moving out of his comfort zone with potentially more money, control, satisfaction and personal growth. However, this came with more risk. The two parts had to be reconciled to satisfy both the logical, conscious part of the brain with the subconscious protective side that was initially fearful of the risks involved. This is quite a visual technique and very effective.

After quite a long session, my client being very resistant and quite cynical about the holding out of his hands, responded very positively. The subconscious mind's fears had been allayed, so that it was now in alignment with the conscious mind. He subsequently went on to form a company with a friend and colleague of many years and took on the groundwork for a large Construction Project. He is now involved in areas of growth he had never been involved in before – interviewing and hiring staff, learning more about IT, Accounts and how business owners operate, leasing and buying large pieces of equipment rather than the old situation where he took no risk and had significantly less responsibility. He has thrived both mentally and emotionally. His self-esteem has increased, and this has been commented on by others also. There have been occasional moments of self-doubt, as is normal and good, to prevent complacency from setting in. This is addressed by an occasional coaching session to enable him maintain focus and to objectively put the considerable progress that has been made, into context. Everything is well on course, however, as due to my doubling up as the Finance Director, I know this to be the case first-hand!

This was a case where he truly stepped out of his comfort zone many times and he now felt much more positive and "light hearted" about the new scenario. He could clearly see the positive benefits to his self-esteem, personal growth and confidence (in addition to the financial rewards) of accepting and succeeding at the challenge. There was now no inner conflict between his subconscious and conscious anymore. There will still be challenges – as with any business – but importantly, there is no inner conflict. It is extremely hard to progress in any venture if there is internal conflict.

The technique has enabled him to resolve the inner conflict that blocked him from starting his business and he was no longer "stuck" but able to take the necessary steps to grow and progress his business. A limited company was formed, staff were hired, and more machinery leased a few weeks later. This in turn has improved both his personal and professional life.

Chapter 4

Need for self-care and high energy strategies

Revisiting the Law of Attraction and high energy levels

At this stage in the journey, it is useful to recap and summarise the Law of Attraction, placing it and strategies for self-care and maintaining high energy levels, into context.

There are general patterns that have been universally ascribed to successful manifestation. In summary, we attract what we put out. If we vibrate at a higher, positive frequency then that is what we will attract back. It could be regarding work, personal relationships, business opportunities – there is an endless list of possibilities. It is also true about our low vibrational thoughts; when we are fearful, resentful, jealous, angry or experiencing feelings of guilt, we attract similarly low frequency things back to us. Abundant thoughts attract abundance into your life. Fate can sometimes throw us a curveball and we can be dealt negative situations such as the death of a loved one or even natural catastrophes. However, we still have power over the meanings we decide to put on those negative situations. The meaning we decide to adopt to explain those situations and the subsequent way in which we deal with them, also have a direct impact on our happiness or unhappiness. Quite often what initially may seem a hopeless situation can serve to strengthen and empower us. We can learn and grow from the experience.

Now that we understand the link between our thoughts and the vibrational frequency that we send out into the universe, it is important to act upon this. We can monitor our thoughts and consciously decide that we will not habitually engage in negative thinking because we know this attracts lack into our lives instead of abundance. It is vital that we understand and deliberately incorporate this fundamental concept into our daily lives. This is not only for our own success and happiness but also for those around us. By having deliberate self-care strategies of being kind to ourselves and nurturing our minds and bodies, we will be in a more positive and abundant state of mind. Similarly, if we are more aware of when we feel low in energy or we seem to have an imbalance, then we can rebalance our energy across the chakras by using energy healing treatments such as reiki.

Another way in which this knowledge is beneficial for us, is that it can also influence our attitude towards the people that we may want to distance ourselves from. Anyone who we now realise drains our energy, lowers the vibration and who is generally negative would be an example of this. It can help identify why a person always seems to be attracting abusive people into their lives. There is a pattern going on. Once this is understood, that negative pattern can be broken. The person can then move on from their previous mindset, be conscious of the importance of vibrating at a high frequency and be open to form more positive relationships.

Moira Geary (Mind Experts' Academy) has summarised 8 steps that she has noticed her positively manifesting clients all put into action. Moira lists these in: **"8 Principles of Manifesting Abundance that Work!"** and I have summarised this below:

1. Ask

Ask exactly what you want as opposed to asking for what you don't want. Focus and create thoughts at the vibrational frequency of what you want so that you will attract it.

2. Be very specific

To create the correct vibration to attract the specific thing that you want into your life, you must first be very clear and specific about exactly what it is that you want. This can apply to many areas of your life e.g. attracting relationships, money, work, peace of mind or in business. If you are starting up a business, be very specific and do research regarding exactly who your market and ideal clients will be. Also know and believe that your revenue in year 1 is going to be the specific amount that you have planned and visualised. I would also add that planning, forecasting and budgeting have a vital role to play in business and a useful role to play in managing your own personal financial planning too.

3. Believe

Your conscious mind may well want to manifest but it must also be aligned with your subconscious to do this successfully. Misalignment of the two can easily be seen by observing body language, tonality of voice, sensory acuity and language patterns that the person is using. If there is a disconnect between the body language and what the person is saying, then this is a clear indication that deep down that person doesn't really believe in it. If the thought vibration is not aligned, then we cannot attract the vibration of what we want to attract.

A tip to help convince the subconscious is firstly, to imagine what you want to attract. Then associate yourself into the mental image and imagine that you are part of this mental image. Start to see, smell, hear, feel and even taste the successful outcome and enjoy the feelings as if you have already manifested. This association into the mental image of what you want to manifest is very important. As with many things, the more you practice it, then the more aligned you will become. Merely stating the intentions and goals will not work if you don't truly believe it. If your spoken words are at odds with your body language, then you should do some work on yourself or with a coach to become aligned both consciously and subconsciously.

4. Expect the things that you want

Everyone has a subconscious, defensive way of thinking that is setup early in our lives. This mechanism serves to warn us about taking certain choices that may result in our feeling sad or disappointed in ourselves if we fail. As well as protecting us, this inner voice can sometimes result in our not progressing in life, career or business because we fear failure so much. The vibration of that fearful thought process is not conducive to attracting what you want. The only way to attract it, is to expect it.

5. Be in abundance and be open to receiving

We need to feel worthy to receive, to be able to feel abundant and to create a vibration that will attract abundance. By being open to receiving, we can create a vibration that will attract abundance of like-minded people, business and life opportunities, happiness, better health or even material wealth into our lives. Like attracts like. We may feel unworthy due to situations, experiences or conditioning from our past childhood. These blocks can be removed as we discussed in Chapter 3 to then free us up to being abundant.

We all deserve to be rich and abundant in every aspect of our lives. Remember that we were born with that right even if somewhere along the line we decided to misalign it.

A common subconscious pattern is that you can receive so long as you give something in return. The underlying belief and conditioning being that it is "greedy" to get more than you give. Vibrating at a frequency of abundance is important. Otherwise, for example, you can generate great business and income, but your monthly outgoings will always match your income, as you may feel that you somehow don't deserve to be making this amount of money or generating such wealth. Another example is Lotto winners. They can sometimes win substantial amounts of money but within a few years have nothing. The mind is very powerful, and it is important to recognise the subconscious beliefs that we hold and how they influence our behaviour and the ultimate outcomes in our lives.

6. Affirm with feeling

Affirmations are dealt with later in this chapter but essentially, they are positive statements made in the present tense and they relate to you and what you plan to achieve.

To be effective, the affirmations must be felt and not merely spoken. Associating yourself into the statement and mental image so that you can see, taste, hear, smell and importantly, really feel that sensation has a much more powerful impact. Tune into the feeling of living the affirmation as you are saying it.

7. Never decide "how" it's going to happen

Having implemented the above actions, it is important not to get hung up and fearful or frustrated about how you will manifest your desired outcome. Fear will block manifestation. Trusting in yourself and the universe is a better approach. If you are taking the necessary actions, it is quite extraordinary how things manifest, even if not in the way you imagined.

8. Remember to say, "thank you"

Practising gratitude for all the things and people that you have manifested in your life is an effective way to align yourself. (For me personally, I generally try to do this upon waking each morning. It puts a lot of things into perspective and has a positive impact on my mood and motivation for the day ahead).

As Moira Geary states, these 8 steps are not "Rocket Science, just Quantum Science". Practising them will set you well on your way to making dramatic changes in your happiness and in your life.

When we feel aligned i.e. healthy, positive, vibrating at an elevated level and feeling good about life – that is without doubt, a wonderful place to be in. However, getting to that point is a skill. Most of us work hard, do the best we can and sometimes feel that we are not enjoying life to the full and are just about getting there. This applies to both men and women alike. However, the law of attraction really does work. Like everything else in life, practice makes perfect and we are creating positive neural pathways each time we practise gratitude and positively visualise and affirm the desired goals we wish to manifest.

We cannot effectively care or contribute fully unless we look after ourselves first. A worn out, depressed person is not likely to contribute much, nor inspire confidence in friends, family or workmates or even feel good within themselves. This notion of "self-care" for women used to be classed as "selfishness" but it is common sense. It's the same advice on planes saying to parents to put on their life jackets first and then attend to their children. Different societies have not been kind to mothers. Huge expectations have been placed upon their shoulders. In prior years in Western society, the roles were more distinct, albeit more restrictive for the married woman. Today, traditional caring duties and responsibilities in addition to success in careers are expected of women. There is also the pressure to maintain youthful attractiveness constantly being reinforced by aggressive advertising and marketing campaigns on mainstream and social media. These campaigns constantly bombard women, especially young girls, to look "perfect" and are designed to exploit and cash-in on our insecurities. In fact, body dysmorphia is increasingly prevalent among young, naturally beautiful young women who are constantly comparing themselves to the surgically enhanced, unnatural looking "role models" who promote artificial and expensive procedures causing them to feel hugely insecure as a result.

A huge "superwoman" expectation exists, that is not only illogical but is detrimental to women if they feel that they must excel at every level on the work, domestic and social front. **Doing the very best that you can is a much kinder approach to yourself than being a perfectionist and being continually disappointed. No one is perfect**. There are obviously huge advantages and disadvantages to be gained from having a job or career. It does need to be tempered by understanding how to deal with the additional workload and criticism so that life can still be enjoyable. That is not to say that women in other parts of the world are not even more impacted. It is now generally accepted that the most effective way to help develop societies is by the inclusion of girls and women in the education process. It is also significant to observe societies that actively and brutally prevent girls and women from being educated, tend to be less happy and successful with more widespread aggression, violence and war.

How many young women play golf for example? Not many are able to, due to time and financial constraints. There are generally more time pressures on working women with children than on their male counterparts. Golf is mainly played by men of all ages, rarely so by younger, working mothers.

So why is that?

I know in my own case the weekends were a time to catch up on housework and shopping. Eventually, as my career progressed, and my disposable income increased, I had my children. I paid to get help with childcare and domestic chores. It appears to be somehow more acceptable that men are entitled to have their "me time" but this is not automatically something that applies to their spouses or partners. We need to address this ourselves as women, especially working women. Having increased demands on our time, we should insist that we also get enough time for ourselves aside from working, doing domestic chores and caring for families. My golf is still very much a work-in-progress by the way – but I am improving! My point being that no way could I have even attempted to play golf until very recently when I had more time.

Simply put, distinct roles and increasing responsibilities were ascribed to women over time, but amazingly and unfairly, they were still expected to be the main carer and to take on ever increasing onerous roles as they enjoyed the success in their careers. Society has the expectation that women actively work outside the home but there is also an expectation that they bear the brunt of domestic chores, raising families and looking after ageing parents. Is this situation fair? No, of course not. Women themselves need to change their behaviours and not necessarily by taking up golf. Women need to put value on themselves and their time and insist and assert that this right should be recognised. It is time to make that change by shifting your own views to believe and reflect this truth. My time is valued amongst most of my circle, but occasional reminders need to be given. Those who consistently do not value my time are soon not in my circle. Women fortunately, are increasingly realising the importance of their self-worth.

You cannot run on empty and it is up to you to call a halt. Everyone else will be quite happy to let you at it, be it work, partner, family, whoever or whatever. Not everyone thinks like this and not everyone is out to use you, but many do. Consequently, there are many women who are totally exhausted and have no time left for themselves at all.

Women working and caring for a younger family particularly, need to care for themselves. It took me a while to come to this realisation, but the penny finally dropped, fortunately. After a lifetime of working long hours, being under constant deadlines, being the major carer for my children (and husband!), ensuring that my Alzheimer afflicted mother's nursing home fees were paid, I still climbed the career ladder but at a cost to myself. I never had any real time to step back and relax. Only on holidays, when I chilled out after a few days, could I step back and have a good look at my life – critically. It was not good. It was all work and stress with not enough time for enjoyment. In fact, the laptop went with me on holidays regularly. I remember taking an unplanned 3-hour phone call from the European H.O. of a company I was working for whilst on holidays in Tenerife. This scenario does not apply to every working woman, but it applies to many and it is like a guilty secret. Men have pressures too but generally working women with children have more.

I have an extremely strong work ethic as do many people. My parents were both teachers and were particularly inspiring. My mother, Catherine Donlon, was born in County Longford in Ireland and got a scholarship to secondary school. Free education should be a right that everyone is entitled to. However, this was certainly not the case back then. Had my mother not got the scholarship to a second level school, the Convent of Mercy in Longford, she probably would not have received a second level education. She got free board during the week which was undoubtedly a great bonus for her parents and five siblings.

Admittedly, times have changed since then. She went on to win the Longford county scholarship to go to the university in Galway, Ireland, graduating in 1933. That was a groundbreaking achievement for its time for a female in Ireland. After graduating, as she could get no work in Ireland, she emigrated to England with no family, friends or connections over there whatsoever. She was completely on her own and with Britain about to declare to join World War 2 in 1939, I can only imagine how much she was cautioned against this move by fearful family and friends. She was an intelligent, ground breaking, independent woman who got her first teaching post in Gerrard's Cross in Buckinghamshire and eventually moved up to the North East of England, living in Redcar. For most of her working life she taught in St. Mary's Convent, Saltersgill in Middlesbrough. She loved her time in Middlesbrough and said it was the first time she had ever felt at home in England. The friendliest people on earth are in the North East of England, both she and I believe.

Had she stayed in Ireland she would not have had such a long and successful career and would have had to resign from teaching when she got married. That Irish law (the "marriage ban") which banned married women from working in the public sector was only completely lifted in 1973. It had been lifted earlier in 1958 for teachers. At that stage (1958) my mother had already enjoyed a 25-year teaching career in England. She taught until she was 62 years old and then both my parents retired to Moydow in Co. Longford, Ireland.

I moved to Ireland in 1978 from the UK after graduating from Durham University, completely unaware of this discriminatory law but was slightly puzzled as to why women were absent from so many careers. The less than proactive attitude towards working women I encountered with many audit clients when training in the early days of my own career in Dublin, has now been put into context.

I am very proud of my mother, her intelligence, passion and bravery. I will call her the "Legend from Longford"! She knew her self-worth and proved this by having a very satisfying and successful career, as did my father, both having had a real vocation to teach. There is nothing as gratifying as talking to now grown adults, whom my parents taught and who speak very highly of them both. They tell me that they were very inspired by them.

Why is all this relevant?

It is relevant because it demonstrates that my mother had a strong belief in herself, had a courageous, positive attitude and a willingness to step out of her comfort zone. She wanted to pursue a professional career and that was quite unusual for a young girl in Ireland at that time. Her natural abilities and diligence paid off, having won both scholarships to second level (Convent of Mercy, Longford) and then third level to National University of Ireland (NUI) Galway. She had set out her goals and made her plans.

Emigrating to a country on the verge of war, knowing no-one and embarking upon a successful teaching career, all show a positivity, determination and perfectly demonstrates the process of stepping out of several comfort zones enabling her to follow her dreams to achieve her goals. This is a good lesson and a practical example for us all.

It is very important for everyone, especially women, to appreciate what they are worth and even though circumstances may not be as difficult today as they were for my mother then, we can all learn and appreciate the need to respect ourselves highly and go for those goals. Another important learning from my mother's example, is that manifestation requires action too. Everything will not fall into your lap if you do not take any positive action.

My father, Joseph MacRory, also worked extremely hard and was sent to live with an aunt in County Tyrone in Northern Ireland as a very young boy, after his own mother died and his father remarried. He spoke very little about his youth in Middlesbrough, as it was probably quite a traumatic time for him and I was told not to ask by my mother. He had great affection for Tyrone however. His two sisters became nuns, but I also suspect there was an element of charity involved in this too. I was surprised to find an allusion to this when I attended one of my aunt's funerals in Cambridge many years later. The exact words used that caught my attention were that my aunt "had been very good to the Vincent de Paul but then they had been very good to her too, when she was young".

I also remember as a very young child, visiting my father's aunt in County Tyrone, as she was dying. This was the aunt with whom he had stayed as a young boy. My father was crying silently. That was more shocking to me than his aunt dying as I had never seen him cry before, not that I had ever seen anyone dying before either. The aunt had never married so my father as a young boy was living with her and helped her on the farm. They got on very well with all their neighbours, both protestant and catholic alike, helping each other out despite ongoing strains between the two communities at that time.

He was very fond of this aunt and stayed with her on the farm until he trained as a teacher in the North. He was offered a teaching role, surprisingly enough as he was a catholic and the job market discriminated against Catholics in those days, as indeed did the voting system. However, he was unhappy living in such a partisan society, so he headed back to Middlesbrough, in the NE of England to teach there. He also had managed to get offered a trial for Middlesbrough Football Club! Having been drafted into World War 2, I am sure his next years were far from easy. I have photos of him in the Garden of Gethsemane in Jerusalem during the war and one of him with a football team he played in whilst overseas. I still have the little football cup that the team pictured in the photo won. So, he was quite a positive person and did manage to get some sight-seeing and football in as well! He returned to Middlesbrough after the war and met my mother and they eventually got married.

They were both a great inspiration to me being hard-working, intelligent and positive role models. We may have strong work ethics, want the best for ourselves and for our own families but that is not enough. **Perseverance in the face of adversity and a determination to make plans and see them through, taking the necessary action to achieve your goals is a strategy to succeed. Dreams alone without any action just don't cut it.**

Another learning I received (although I possibly did not practise it enough on myself) concerns the need to make the time for our own self-care. Even though my mother worked hard as a relatively older working mother with two children, she visited the hairdresser every fortnight and paid to have help with the housework. She also made sure we all had a six weeks holiday every summer back in Ireland. Ahead of her time, maybe. Then again, she had a career and financial independence. She didn't have to ask my dad if she could go to the hairdressers as she had her own money and car! Being well educated and financially independent is extremely important for girls and women. These are two of my strongest beliefs. Naturally, my father also had long teacher's holidays and he loved visiting Longford for our annual family holiday. My parents, my brother Joe and I all stayed with my mother's brother, uncle Joe and visited other uncles, aunts and cousins who all lived on farms in Ardagh and Moydow in County Longford. We were truly blessed.

We know about the Law of Attraction and understand about high energy levels. It follows therefore, if you are burning yourself out working and caring for everyone else – you are not respecting yourself and will eventually become exhausted with low energy. It makes absolutely no sense (from your own and from everyone else's perspective) not to take loving care of ourselves.

Before I move on to other aspects to help increase our energy levels, I must stress that I believe that it is important that partners and growing children participate in household chores. It is a good learning experience so that they do not become lazy and grow up with unrealistic expectations or feel that they are entitled. If finances allow, it could be helpful to get in some paid help to clean the house or pay the children pocket money when they are old enough to help with chores, instead of them expecting "free" pocket money. This will prepare them for when they too earn their own money in the real world. It will also take some of the pressures off the mothers who are stretched to the limit.

I want to touch on visualisation next, as a useful and effective means in the journey to achieving your dreams and goals. Visualisation is a particularly helpful tool if you are stressed, stuck in a rut and feel that there is no other way out. You can imagine a new and better way of life. By practising effective visualisation, you will create new, positive neural pathways to replace the previous negative beliefs and weaken the old neural pathways associated to them. By then vibrating at a higher level, you are therefore opening yourself to more positive possibilities and manifestation.

Effective Visualisation

When thinking about your dreams and setting your goals, visualisation, as previously stated, is a great technique to practise and reinforce those positive neural pathways. Everybody has the capacity to visualise, even if they have never even consciously done it before and may doubt their ability to do so. You know that you can visualise memories easily enough and create past images of old memories in your mind. Equally, we are therefore capable of creating in our imagination, mental images of future possibilities and positive images of our dreams.

It is easy to visualise any amount of goals, but it will not be effective unless you really feel it deeply within yourself. Below I have outlined an exercise that you can carry out to prove that you are capable of visualisation.

EXERCISE:

- Close your eyes to minimise distractions.
- Remember the last time you walked into your living room.
- Visualise a picture of the entrance – the colour, material and design of the door. Other details in the living room – wall colour, tiled or carpeted floor, wooden furniture etc.
- Practice remembering the image and become more aware of both the image itself and of the feelings it generates. Maybe a feeling of security and safety as you are finally at home and can go in, relax, have something to eat and chill-out after a hard day's work.
- Notice that in recalling the image, the more defined it is and the bigger, brighter, closer (as in a colourful, moving video), the stronger that feeling is.
- The speed of the video, the focus, nearness and colours are all sub-modalities. By ramping them up, you can get a clearer, more positive and vivid image. (Much the same as when we did the exercise on "anchoring").

Now that you know you can visualise the past, you also know you can visualise the future.

Visualisation is important because when we create thoughts or images in our head then a neurological response is created. From this response, feelings are also created and associated with the image. Messages pass through the nerve cells by electrical impulses when these feelings are created. If the pattern is reinforced, then our nervous system sets up a cybernetic loop between our thoughts, which then will trigger the desired positive feelings. The associated feelings cause us to behave in certain ways. We can use this knowledge to visualise into the future of when our goals and dreams are achieved, imagining that we have already achieved them and how this makes us feel.

By ramping up the positive mental image, the associated feelings can become more intense. This is extremely useful for using on your vision board. Run some of the images on it as if they are colourful films and so enhance their power and the associated feelings. Associate yourself into the film so that you are feeling it. Remember that what we feel is what we can manifest. By feeling that you have already achieved these goals, then you are creating positive neural pathways that are reinforced each time you perform this exercise.

Another use of visualisation is to delete negative mental pictures or images. Often depressed people are concentrating on negative images, so the loop keeps looping to reinforce the negative image and triggers associated negative feelings. By toning down the sub-modalities and making the image blurred, black and white, non-moving, far away image with no sound, you can minimise or delete the associated negative feelings altogether. This will also weaken that negative neural pathway. Replace the negative image with a positive one instead so you can generate positive feelings in their place.

Athletes and sports people frequently use visualisation to improve their performance. If you focus on the positive aspects of visualising a great drive in golf, it is far more likely that you will think positively which then influences positive behaviour and results. It is much more effective to positively visualise the actual golf swing, a good connection, where you will land the ball and plan your shots rather than focussing on the negatives and fearfully concentrating on bunkers, rivers, lakes or whatever hazards there are. I am thinking especially of Lisheen Springs Golf Club in Brittas, County Dublin here, especially holes 13,14 and 15 in my case! Clearly, all the previously mentioned obstacles will have been factored in when planning the golf drive, but the real focus should then be on the positive outcome. When I use this approach to my golf drive, it generally works. Alternatively, if I am fearful and hold back, I land the ball in all the hazards that I am fearful about!

Practice visualisations on your vision board and in any sports that you engage in. If you are in low spirits, visualise an image that makes you feel good. By practising daily, the technique will become easier.

Positive visualisation can be used to make us feel good as an alternative to another glass of wine, another piece of cake or a cigarette. It is a profound and simple tool, which is very easy to implement to quickly elevate our mood.

EXERCISES:

1. **Visualise yourself engaging in activities that you used to enjoy** but no longer participate in. This may be due to family, financial or work commitments but a lot of enjoyable activities cost very little or are even free. In my case tennis, reading and swimming are all things I enjoy. I never stopped reading but did stop the tennis and swimming for quite a while. I have addressed both now. Another visualisation could also be of the outcome of eating healthier. Imagine a fitter, slimmer, healthier, happier, more energised you and the good feelings that this brings.

2. **Explore negative reasons for not doing these things** – are they valid reasons or just excuses? You should exercise for several reasons including purely making time for yourself. It does not need to cost much. Sport enhances fitness and increases dopamine levels (a feel-good hormone) – so sport is good for you mentally as well as physically. Walking in the fresh air is free. The fitter physically and mentally you are, then the better able you will be to mind yourself and family, elderly parents and to interact more positively with partners, friends, work colleagues and the community. Visualise a healthier, fitter lifestyle and the positive results that will follow – a happier, healthier, fitter you with higher energy and capacity to deal with physical and mental challenges.

3. **Use positive visualisation to feel good regularly**. To effectively and positively visualise you need to associate yourself into the visualisation so that you are part of it. You are in the picture – associated into it and feel it, as opposed to being disassociated from it and looking in from the outside. This theme of being associated comes up frequently as we saw earlier in anchoring, here in visualisation and as you will see in affirmations, later in this chapter.

4. An effective way to use visualisation is to **work daily on your Vision Board** and associate yourself into some of your dreams and visions on the board.

Diet and Nutrition

"Diet" refers to the types and amounts of foods that we eat. It is not just a term in relation to someone being "on a diet" so that they lose weight. "Nutrition" is about eating a healthy and balanced diet resulting in the body absorbing the correct balance of the required nutrients such as proteins, vitamins, minerals, carbohydrates so that we grow and maintain a healthy life.

A good diet includes a balance of several different food groups. Each of these food groups supplies the different nutrients that our body requires for maintenance, repair and growth. The main food groups are carbohydrates, fruit and vegetables, protein, dairy, fats and sugars:

1. **Carbohydrates:** This group includes wholegrains and sugars such as bread, pasta, cakes and cereals. Wholegrain varieties are the healthiest varieties to eat as refined or processed carbohydrates such as white bread and pastries cause inflammation. There is more on inflammation later in this section. Natural sweeteners such as honey and stevia are preferable to refined white sugar. Too much sugar can lead to weight gain, heart problems, type 2 diabetes caused by blood sugar imbalance and many other health issues. The recommended maximum daily intake of sugar is 9 teaspoons by the American Heart Association (AHA) but 7 teaspoons by the UK Government Scientific Advisory Committee on Nutrition (SACN). Sugar is added to many foods. A 330 ml can of fizzy drink alone contains 35g/9 teaspoons of free sugar.

2. **Fruits and Vegetables:** Those vegetables which are rich in vitamins, minerals and fibre offer protection against heart disease, type 2 diabetes and cancer. Coloured vegetables have huge health benefits and the following chart shows summary detail regarding "Pigments, Roles in Plants and Value to Humans". This chart is reproduced from "Living Naturally" by Margaret Boyles. Natural, unprocessed fruits and vegetables are the easiest for our bodies to digest and so we retain more nutrients than from tinned or processed sources. Fruit contains naturally occurring sugar in the form of fructose, so consider your overall sugar intake as well. Whole fruits are much preferable to concentrated fruit juices that are exceptionally high in sugar and can be consumed so easily without realising that this is the case.

Pigment class	Indicative colours	Roles in plants	Foods rich in these pigments	Potential value to humans
Chlorophyll (fat-soluble)	Green	harvest light; initiate photosynthesis	green vegetables	help deactivate carcinogens
Carotenoids (fat-soluble	red-orange-yellow	attract pollinators and seed dispersers accessory photosynthetic pigment in periods of low light, absorbs excess light energy, antioxidant roles, substrate for hormones	carrot, sweet potato, winter squash, pumpkin, green leafy vegetables, cantaloupe, apricot	Protect the immune system, skin, epithelial cells. Prevent heart disease, cancer and macular degeneration.
Anthocyanins (water-soluble: don't throw out cooking water)	blue-purple-burgundy-	attract pollinators and seed dispersers repel predators, protect cells from damage by excess light, improve plant tolerance to stress such as drought, UV-B, and heavy metals, resist disease, scavenge free radicals.	purple vegetables (onions, cabbage, potatoes), red, blue & purple berries, black beans	prevent, forestall, possibly even reverse age-related cognitive declines and neuro-degenerative diseases; improve night vision and other vision disorders, protect against heart disease, insulin resistance, cancer; promote wound healing
Betalains (water-soluble)	red, yellow	powerful antioxidant	beets (red and yellow), chard, spinach, fruit of prickly-pear cactus	Antioxidant may protect against heart disease, various cancers, ulcers, liver damage

3. **Protein** is an extremely important type of food group as it builds and repairs tissues in the body. Hair and nails are mainly made up of protein. It is also used to make enzymes, hormones and other body chemicals. Protein is an important building block of bones, muscles, cartilage, skin and blood. Excellent sources of protein include meat, fish and eggs. Vegetarian sources of protein include beans, nuts and soya. Protein-rich foods often contain higher levels of minerals such as iron, magnesium, potassium and zinc. These **minerals** are essential for healthy living also.

- **Iron**: Half the iron in our bodies is in the red blood cells. It is an important part of the protein known as haemoglobin, responsible for carrying oxygen to the tissues in our body. This enables energy to be released and allows our bodies to carry out its necessary functions. Iron also forms part of other proteins and enzymes critical to effective body functions.

- **Magnesium**: This is required for hundreds of chemical reactions in our bodies. 60% resides in the body's bones with the remaining 40% in muscles and soft tissues. Some of the chemical reactions that magnesium is required for, include:

  - ❖ Controlling blood glucose levels and pressure
  - ❖ Proper functioning of muscles, nerves and brain
  - ❖ Energy metabolism and protein production

- **Zinc**: Is essential for proper growth and development during pregnancy, childhood and adolescence. It plays a role in:

  - ❖ Protein synthesis
  - ❖ Immune system function
  - ❖ Wound healing
  - ❖ DNA synthesis (replicating our genetic blueprint in cells as we grow)

- **Potassium**: This is required for muscle contraction, proper heart function, transmission of nerve signals and for some enzyme functions.

4. **Dairy:** This group includes milk, yoghurt and cheese. Dairy foods provide a rich source of calcium that is necessary for healthy bones and teeth.

5. **Fats:** Fats are important for brain health, energy, absorption of certain vitamins, skin, hair and joint health. There are two sorts of fat, saturated and unsaturated.

    a) **Saturated fats** are present in foods such as cream, fatty meat and fried food. If eaten in excess, they can lead to heart disease.

    b) **Unsaturated fats** are present in oily fish, nuts and avocado to name a few examples. Unsaturated fats help to reduce the cholesterol produced by the saturated fats in our blood. The World Health Organisation (WHO) recommends that unsaturated fats make up 30% of a person's total calories intake. High cholesterol levels in the blood is a risk factor associated with heart disease.

There is generally a consensus regarding what are the overall quantities in which the above food groups should be eaten to achieve a healthy and well-balanced diet. The food pyramid is a common tool to visually demonstrate what the healthy portions in each food group should be.

My own personal view is that whilst I love the Mediterranean-style model and have a natural preference for foods that are anti-inflammatory, I also think it is very important to enjoy your food. So many of our bonding rituals with partners, family and friends involve enjoying the tastes, visual presentation and aromas of our food along with the pleasure of good company and laughter. The levels of the pleasure hormone, dopamine, increases, and our energy vibration rises when there is genuine positive engagement around savouring appetising and healthy culinary delights in enjoyable company.

The proliferation of food disorders fractures the genuine enjoyment of eating and savouring the tastes and aromas of natural, healthy food. There has always been an acknowledgement throughout history and different societies that strong positive bonds are formed when sharing food and relaxing with friends and loved ones.

Much misinformation exists about food in many marketing strategies that are rolled out on mainstream and social media. The aim is purely to exploit insecurities and create anxieties, or "pain points", for the sole purpose of selling products. The facts are being obscured by the desire to make money. Health concerns are often not at the forefront of many marketing campaigns regarding both food and pharmaceuticals. So often, there are many natural, holistic treatments readily available without resorting to artificially produced chemicals. The natural, holistic remedies are cheaper and kinder to our bodies and wellbeing. They do not trigger the negative side effects caused by the artificially produced alternatives that contain additives. Our bodies cannot easily digest the artificial additives resulting in inflammation, the cause of many modern diseases.

The "diet" industry is notorious for inventing pseudo-scientific terms that are designed to add credibility to some of the ludicrous claims that are made regarding their products. It is also to justify higher prices for dietary products than for ordinary brands. Another very unhelpful aspect is the incorrect demonisation of fat. Unsaturated fat is a necessary part of a nutritious diet so long as it is not overdone (30% is recommended by the WHO). Replacing it with added sugar and artificial sweeteners (as in so many of the processed foods) is harmful to our health. This addition of sugar is often masked by the "Low Fat" banner. Check out the sugar content in so-called diet foods. Yoghurts are a case in point. Obesity is rife in Western societies such as Ireland, the UK and US. However, sugar is a money-spinner, so is not being exposed as the threat to our health that it really poses. Powerful lobbies and industries want to keep it this way because it is an extremely profitable commodity. Check out how much sugar is in your breakfast cereal. You may be quite surprised. The good news is that there is increasingly more awareness building up of the dangers of too much sugar in our diets and sugar taxes are being introduced in many countries.

In Ireland, a commitment made to introduce a sugar tax by 2018, using the same structure as the UK legislation, has been honoured. This is good news. However, it will also dent the huge profits of the companies promoting their sugar-laden products who are clearly more interested in making profit than tackling the nation's increasing obesity levels. Sugar sells and lobbying against effective taxation of sugar is ongoing. At least first steps have been taken.

The first "Healthy Eating Pyramid" was developed in Sweden in the 1970s as a simple conceptual model to introduce the idea of healthy eating. Since then there have been a myriad of food pyramids produced as research and more insights became available. The food pyramids are easy to understand as they visually display the different food groups (with specific food examples) in the desired proportions for a balanced and healthy diet.

However, as knowledge and research has increased, there has been an evolution in thinking as to what are the optimal proportions of each food groups that make up a healthy diet. I have included three food pyramids in the following pages to show how this thinking has evolved. I have deliberately selected the Mediterranean food pyramid which has consistently been universally acknowledged as a healthy, nutritional food model. More recently we became aware of the "glycaemic index" and the role of "inflammation" in the increase of cancers, so I have included food pyramids that include details on these areas also.

The **"Mediterranean Diet"** as represented in the following food pyramid has long been acknowledged as being particularly healthy as borne out by many studies. The Mayo Clinic in the US has stated "the Mediterranean diet is associated with a reduced incidence of cancer, Parkinson's and Alzheimer's diseases. Women who eat a Mediterranean diet supplemented with extra-virgin olive oil and mixed nuts may have a reduced risk of breast cancer".

This "Traditional Healthy Mediterranean Diet Pyramid" has been developed by Oldways Preservation and Exchange Trust.

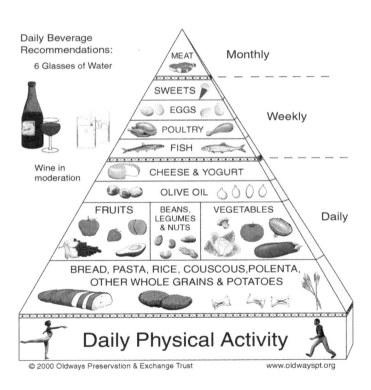

More research into better diets and nutrition has revealed the importance of limiting the consumption of food with a high "glycaemic" index. The "Glycaemic Index" (G.I.) is a value assigned to foods based on how slowly (the preferred option) or quickly those foods cause increases in blood sugar or glucose levels. The lower G.I. diets are associated with decreased risk of a vast array of conditions from cardiovascular diseases and type 2 diabetes to gall stones, depression, uterine fibroids and cancers of the breast, colon and prostrate. Whole, natural and non-processed foods including herbs and spices have either a low or very low G.I.

The **"New Food Pyramid"** shown below, includes this G.I. concept and has been produced by the US Department of Agriculture (USDA). This has expanded the four food groups of the original Swedish Food Pyramid to six food groups and varied the portion sizes. It educates people to eat a more balanced diet from a greater variety of food portions without counting calories. It is more flexible, as if you are trying to lose weight, you can select the lower portion sizes within the recommend range

Finally, the last food pyramid I have chosen is the most comprehensive of the three and gives practical guidance in addition to illustrating the desirable quantities within each of the food groups.

This is the **"TUI Heights Healthy Food"** Pyramid developed in New Zealand and is reproduced below.

Tui Heights Healthy Food Pyramid

- Eat sensibly — use common sense
- Avoid extremes
- Eat homemade
- Eat home grown or organic when you can
- Limit or avoid processed & junk foods
- Avoid artificial sweeteners & sugar
- Avoid most vegetable oils & ALL margarine

Dairy
Consume small volumes of healthy whole, raw or fermented dairy products including raw milk, yoghurt & cheese

Protein
Include healthy sources including wild salmon, fresh fish, free range & grass fed chicken, turkey, beef, lamb, pork & eggs

Water
Plenty of clean, fresh, non-fluoridated water

Grains & Sugars
Minimal to no consumption of simple sugars & carbohydrates. Include small volumes of ancient grains, whole grains & natural healthy sweeteners like honey, stevia, xylitol. Very small volumes of muscovado or demerara unrefined sugar is ok too—for most people.

Legumes
Include small volumes of appropriately prepared legumes—i.e. soaked, sprouted, fermented

Herbs & Spices
Include plenty of herbs & spices especially turmeric, cinnamon and Himalayan salt

Fruits
Consume in moderation
2—3 serves daily

Healthy Fats
Include moderate amounts of healthy fats including coconut oil, butter, beef dripping or lard, extra virgin olive oil, avocado & raw nuts

Vegetables
Consume lots of fresh, lightly cooked & raw vegetables
5—8 serves daily

"Medical News Today", gives other tips for eating a healthy and nutritious diet that include the following:

1. Manage portion size

People of different ages, genders and activity levels need different amounts of food, but many people take in more energy than they use. Researchers believe there is a link between portion size and obesity. The American Heart Association (AHA) explain that a "portion" is what we choose to eat, while a "serving" (as in the food pyramids above) is the amount of food listed on the food label. Examples of servings are one slice of bread and one wedge of melon. Paying attention to what a serving is, how many calories are in a serving and how much you are eating can make the difference between obesity and maintaining a healthy diet.

2. Eat fresh and avoid processed food

Processed foods make up 70% of the average American diet. Fresh foods are more likely to be "nutrient rich" whilst processed foods are often "energy rich" with added fats and sugars. Whole foods such as fresh fruit and vegetables are also a source of vitamins and minerals. Processed foods not only contain added ingredients including dyes and preservatives, but the processing itself can destroy nutrients. Some processed foods contain little nutritional value. Consuming a high proportion of processed foods can increase the risk of heart disease and diabetes.

3. Limit added sugars

Naturally occurring sugars include fructose, as found in fruit and lactose, as is found in dairy products. Adding sugars to food and drink enhances flavour but adds little or no nutritional value. Swapping cakes and cookies for fruit and reducing the sugar added to tea and coffee can reduce sugar intake. Replacing fizzy drinks with sparkling water and reducing alcohol intake can also help reduce excess calories. Condiments such as ketchup have sugar added to them as do almost all processed food.

4. Replace animal fats in the diet

Animal produce is often high in saturated fats. Saturated fats are difficult for the body to break down so that the level of harmful cholesterol in the body can rise, potentially leading to heart disease.

As mentioned, unsaturated fats as in avocado, nuts and oily fish are a healthier alternative to red meat. Red meat should always be eaten in moderation.

To reduce the amount of unhealthy fat in the diet:

- Use low-fat meat
- Cook meat and chicken without the skin
- Grill or boil meat instead of frying
- Use vegetable fat instead of animal fat
- Replace some meat servings with oily fish, nuts, beans or legumes

5. Add calcium and vitamin D

Calcium is crucial for strengthening and maintain the bone structure. Vitamin D helps the body to store calcium. Sources of calcium include:
   a. Dairy produce
   b. Soya beans
   c. White beans

6. Dietary sources do not provide enough vitamin D for the body

Sunlight is necessary to help the body synthesise vitamin D. Exposing some bare skin to the sunlight each day will help maintain levels of calcium and vitamin D.

7. **An active lifestyle involving exercise combined with a healthy diet**

A combination of healthy diet and exercise will produce the best results. I deal with exercise and the proportional impact of diet and exercise (in relation to losing weight) in the next section.

We may be aware of the importance of a healthy diet but can quite frequently skip meals or overindulge in comfort eating when we are feeling a little stressed or upset. It is best to try and plan to have healthy foods readily available so that we are stocked up for such stressful times. Planning healthy lunches for work and trying to go for a lunchtime walk are other effective tools to help you.

Another more recent development in research into diet, is the concept of "inflammation". This occurs when the body's immune system attacks anything in the body that it recognises as foreign. It could be an invading microbe, plant pollen or a chemical. Intermittent bouts of inflammation as a response to genuinely threatening invaders are necessary and good as it protects our health. If the inflammation is continually experienced where there is no threat, then it becomes our enemy and causes cancers, heart disease, diabetes, arthritis, depression and Alzheimer's disease.

Dr. Frank Hu, previously professor of nutrition and epidemiology in the Department of Nutrition at the Harvard School of Public Health, comments that "many experimental studies have shown that components of foods or beverages may have anti-inflammatory effects. Some of the foods that have been associated with an increased risk for chronic diseases such as type 2 diabetes and heart disease are also associated with excess inflammation".

Significantly however, he also highlights that "some of the food components or ingredients may have independent effects on inflammation over and above increased calorific intake." Choosing the right foods can therefore reduce your risk of illness. Consistently picking the wrong types of food will most likely accelerate the inflammatory disease process.

The foods that combat inflammation are:

- Tomatoes
- Olive oil
- Green leafy vegetables
- Nuts like almonds and walnuts
- Fatty fish
- Fruits such as strawberries, cherries, oranges and blueberries

Not surprisingly, the foods that cause inflammation are:

- Refined carbohydrates such as white bread and pastries
- French fries or chips and other fried foods
- Soda and other sugar-sweetened beverages
- Red meat especially processed burgers and sausages
- Margarine and lard

I am an avid fan of organic food and indeed grew organic strawberries commercially (on a small basis) for five years in the 1990s in addition to working as an accountant and consultant. My customers over a five-year period included Superquinn, Tesco and local restaurants. Finally, I sold my strawberries directly to the public from a stall in the Temple Bar market, Dublin, on Saturday mornings over the summer months. It was huge fun selling at a market and my young children sometimes came with me!

Organic produce is not subject to all the antibiotics and chemicals that have been used on non-organic fruit, vegetables and animal produce. Besides therefore being better for your health (as these chemicals can produce inflammation), there is such a difference in taste between organic and non-organic food. The organic produce is normally much fresher as there are no chemicals to artificially prolong shelf-life. Organic food is also easier to digest, as it contains only natural ingredients and in the case of my organic strawberries – as many have agreed, looked, tasted and smelled much better than the non-organic ones. Elderly ladies especially, used to tell me that the taste of my organic strawberries reminded them of the way strawberries used to taste when they were young girls. How good is that?

There is a current debate as to whether organic produce is value for money or not. If you were aware first-hand of all the chemicals that can be (and are being) used on commercially grown non-organic strawberries (and other non-organic fruit and vegetables), you might just reconsider your viewpoint. I attended a Strawberry Conference in Wexford, specifically organised for strawberry growers by Teagasc (the Irish national body providing research, advisory and training services to the agricultural and food industry). It was shocking to see the large lists of approved herbicides and pesticides that were being routinely applied within commercial strawberry production. Another significant observation was the list of chemicals that had just recently been banned by the EU. The general response of the growers seemed to be more of disappointment rather than of appreciating that these chemicals were banned due to the underlying negative impact on our health. This was back in the late 90's and the fact that I was the only organic strawberry grower in attendance was treated with incredulity and a little bit of rudeness. Each to their own!

Attitudes to organic produce have changed since then fortunately. Increasingly more of these harmful chemicals are being banned every year as they are proven scientifically to not only be bad for our health, but some were even found to be carcinogenic. The range of more sensibly priced organic fruit and vegetables currently available today is testament to this. Lidl stock a good range of reasonably priced organic produce and some Irish supermarkets are increasingly following this trend.

A healthy diet obviously involves a balanced mix of nutrients, cutting down on (or even cutting out) processed food, fried foods, sugars, fizzy drinks, cakes and junk food if possible. Smoking is a proven killer, so it makes sense to try and break this habit. There are a lot of facilities available for people who want to give up smoking such as hypnotism, Health Service Executive (HSE) programmes in Ireland or nicotine patches to name but a few. Reducing alcohol, caffeine, salt and increasing fresh fruit and especially fresh vegetables is also a good move. Drinking plenty of water daily to keep hydrated plus adding a sprig of mint or some pure lemon juice for flavour is also an attractive bonus.

Meat is a reliable source of protein and cutting down on red meat due to its high level of saturated fat, as mentioned previously, is now widely accepted to be better for our health. It can be replaced with some white lean meat such as chicken or turkey. Oily fish such as salmon, tuna and anchovies contain natural omega 3 oils are also healthy substitutes. The natural omega oils are essential nutrients which are important in preventing and managing heart disease as well as providing benefits for skin and brain function. Eating more nuts, peas, beans and pulses and vegetables bring more healthy nutrients into our diet as a replacement for the less healthy foods.

Much has been written about the value of supplements and mainly in a negative way. Whether you are young, at the menopausal or post-menopause stage (to my female readers, naturally!), it is worth looking at supplements. The optimal solution is, of course, to obtain your essential nutrients by eating a healthy, balanced diet. There is no doubt that there is overkill and slick marketing to maximise profits and sell false hope to people regarding the benefits of supplements. In some cases, however, taking a supplement may be the best solution.

Osteoporosis is a particularly female affliction that can be avoided by engaging in weight-bearing exercise and eating an adequate amount of calcium in the diet, especially in younger years. Unfortunately, society pressurises an alarming proportion of young girls into negative body image and extreme dieting, so they have not been consuming enough calcium. In some instances, young girls have also not been exercising regularly. As a result, osteoporosis is becoming increasingly more common.

The best way to ensure we have balanced nutrients is obviously via our food intake. If you know you don't have a particularly high calcium intake and are allergic to dairy for example, then maybe use alternatives food sources like kale or else a calcium supplement. It is good to run this by your doctor if there are any medical concerns. I did read about someone many years back who accidently overdosed on carrot juice – so balance in all things is necessary. Seeking medical advice before embarking on an exercise routine after years of no exercise is also advised, especially if you have a medical condition to consider. The next section is all about exercise.

Exercise

Manifestation will be more likely to increase if you undertake regular physical exercise. Exercise increases energy, increases your vibration and increases your physical, mental and emotional wellbeing. It also keeps thoughts and ideas flowing and we find tasks, both mental and physical, easier to do because we have more energy. Even as basic as 20–30 minutes brisk walking three times a week is one of the easiest ways to quickly and cheaply, improve your health. This form of aerobic exercise has been proven and recommended by several cardiologists. Why don't you try and incorporate this small but extremely effective change into your daily life?

If any aerobic exercise at all can be included in your daily routine, this will have a very positive impact. Aerobic exercise includes walking, running, cycling or swimming with a focus on using up oxygen in our cardiovascular system. It increases heart rate and breathing rate so that more blood is pumped around our body to feed oxygen to the muscles. As you become a little short of breath this will also burn calories, so there is a double benefit. There is a vast variety of exercises, gym routines, and sports available today, so take your time and experiment and select the ones you enjoy.

Many people really enjoy running and it makes a real difference in their lives both physically and mentally. One point I have noticed is that running along hard surfaces such as roads can be very bad for your joints, especially when you get older. I know a forty-something who was very fit and health conscious and did a lot of running, daily, throughout his life. Unfortunately, he had to get two hip replacements in his late forties. Like most things, moderation is probably the best practice.

Swimming is another good recommendation, as if you have a weight problem, the water will help to buoy you up so that you can exercise more easily. In fact, there are so many choices – it's just getting around to replacing a bad relaxation habit (comfort food, wine) with a good one (exercise) and one that also raises dopamine levels to lift your mood. It is an excellent idea to do an exercise you like so that it is something to look forward to - be it Zumba, hockey, tennis or exercising in the gym. Similarly, also rope in a friend as an exercise buddy to make exercising easier and more enjoyable.

By thinking positively and therefore acting more positively, we will relax more naturally and will be drawn to adopting healthier options for our leisure time such as sporting activities. Sport involving others, so that it also has an element of social network about it like team sports, golf and tennis clubs, will not only benefit and help your body but will also boost your social activity and therefore further relax your mind. The increase in dopamine which improves your mood level, the feel-good factor, increase in energy and improved health may surprise you if you do get into the habit of a healthy exercise routine.

There are many options available to us today for enjoying exercise. Several on-line courses and DVD programmes exist in additional to the multitude of exercise classes held in traditional gyms. Physical exercise performed outside in nature, is even better for mental and physical health. I have joined a golf club and a tennis club but truthfully, I could never have done this before when I had children and was working long hours. It would have been impossible for me. Then again, perhaps, I should have been delegating more and practicing self-care had I been in possession of the knowledge that I now have.

When engaging upon a weight-loss plan, it has been established that the relative impact of diet versus exercise is 80% diet and 20% exercise. Holly Lofton, M.D., an assistant professor of medicine and director of the weight management programme at New York's University's Langone Medical Centre, states "You can lose weight without exercise, but you cannot lose weight if your nutrition counteracts your energy expenditure through exercise". She continues, "I see this in patients all the time. People think that if they run the marathon or go to boot camp, they will lose weight. They're often very disappointed when they don't." A combination of diet and exercise is best at any stage of weight loss. The exercise should be a mix of strength training and cardiovascular training, not just cardio. Both modes of exercise burn fat and, in turn, lead to stored fat being used as a source of energy.

During the first few weeks of losing weight, a rapid drop is normal. This is partly because you have cut calories and the body gets the energy it needs by releasing its stores of glycogen, a type of carbohydrate found in the muscles and liver. Glycogen contains water so when it is burned it releases this water. The initial weight loss is mainly water however, so the effect is temporary. As you continue to lose weight you also lose muscle as well as fat. Muscle helps to keep your body's metabolism up i.e. the rate at which you burn calories. Also, if you don't exercise, the weight loss you experience will include fat loss but also you will strip away muscle and bone density. The more muscle content your body has (as opposed to fat), then the more effective will the same exercise routine be on your body. Therefore, as you lose weight and muscle, your body's metabolism declines so your weight loss slows. Your body has reached a "Weight loss plateau".

Dr. Holly Lofton comments on experiencing a weight loss plateau - "The body tends to resist weight loss when you start eating less which can lead to a plateau." Even though your body may start to slow down as you lose weight, you can speed it up and overcome a weight loss plateau by working out and especially by strength training. The less fat and the more muscle you have, then your body will be more effective at burning calories.

Consider your schedule and your life. Reassess your habits (have you loosened the rules regarding exercise and diet?). Look at the size of the portions you consume and try to pack more activity into the day by using stairs not lifts, walking more by using the car less, vigorous spring cleaning and any other physical activity that can help you to burn more calories. Include planning and cooperation regarding any necessary child support, so you can manage to attend your chosen physical or sporting activities. Devoting time for yourself in this way is a healthy outlet and decreases stress levels.

I have recently taken up yoga and find it helps me to meditate, relax and exercise. I had tried meditation several years ago but found it very hard to meditate on my own. I realised that yoga can help me meditate and both relax my mind as well as my body. It leaves me feeling refreshed and energised after a session. I have also discovered Reiki – thanks to Reiki Master Trudy Ryan of Ballina in County Tipperary – and that is amazing for relaxing, realigning your energies and for a mental, spiritual and emotional recharge. Reiki can make a huge difference to your life. Practising reiki on yourself can help you to ensure that your energy levels and chakras are balanced at any time. Reiki can also be sent to others once you are trained to do this. The ability to help others by sending healing energy is an additional attraction for me.

It is most definitely worth persevering with trying to meditate. If I had realised how good meditation is on so many levels, I would have taken it up much earlier in my life with more commitment. It quietens a racing mind and grounds you. The breathing exercises, "Buddha breathing", where you inhale deeply – without raising your shoulders – instead extending your stomach to your diaphragm and allow your lungs to fill up more is excellent for relaxing and improving the lymphatic system.

Meditation

The following article is the best summary that I have come across regarding the benefits of meditation and the underlying scientific bases for these conclusions. I used to consider Meditation a bit "out there" but since educating myself a bit more on the subject and appreciating first-hand the benefits of meditation, especially combined with practising yoga and reiki, I am truly a convert and my cynicism is completely gone.

"Meditation has 7 main health benefits by Alice G Walton.

1.   Meditation Reduces Activity in the Brain's "Me Center"

Last week, a _study_ from UCLA found that long-term meditators had better-preserved brains than non-meditators as they aged. Participants who'd been meditating for an average of 20 years had more grey matter volume throughout the brain – although older meditators still had some volume loss compared to younger meditators, it wasn't as pronounced as the non-meditators. "We expected rather small and distinct effects located in some of the regions that had previously been associated with meditating," said study author Florian Kurth. "Instead, what we actually observed was a widespread effect of meditation that encompassed regions throughout the entire brain."

One of the most interesting _studies_ in the last few years, carried out at _Yale University_, found that mindfulness meditation decreases activity in the default mode network (DMN), the brain network responsible for mind-wandering and self-referential thoughts – a.k.a., "monkey mind." The DMN is "on" or active when we're not thinking about anything, when our minds are just wandering from thought to thought. Since mind-wandering is typically _associated with being less happy_, ruminating, and worrying about the past and future, it's the goal for many people to dial it down. Several studies have shown that meditation, though its quieting effect on the DMN, appears to do just this. And even when the mind does start to wander, because of the new connections that form, meditators are better at snapping back out of it.

2.   Its Effects Rival Antidepressants for Depression, Anxiety

A review _study_ last year at Johns Hopkins looked at the relationship between mindfulness meditation and its ability to reduce symptoms of depression, anxiety, and pain. Researcher Madhav Goyal and his team found that the effect size of meditation was moderate, at 0.3. If this sounds low, keep in mind that the effect size for antidepressants is also 0.3, which makes the effect of meditation sound good. Meditation is, after all an active form of brain training. "A lot of people have this idea that meditation means sitting down and doing nothing," says Goyal. "But *that's not true. Meditation is an active training of the mind to increase awareness, and different meditation programs approach this in different ways." Meditation isn't a magic bullet for depression, as no treatment is, but it's one of the tools that may help manage symptoms.*

3. Meditation May Lead to Volume Changes in Key Areas of the Brain

In 2011, Sara Lazar and her team at Harvard found that mindfulness meditation can actually change the structure of the brain: Eight weeks of Mindfulness-Based Stress Reduction (MBSR) was found to increase cortical thickness in the hippocampus, which governs learning and memory, and in certain areas of the brain that play roles in emotion regulation and self-referential processing. There were also decreases in brain cell volume in the amygdala, which is responsible for fear, anxiety, and stress – and these changes matched the participants' self-reports of their stress levels, indicating that meditation not only changes the brain, but it changes our subjective perception and feelings as well. In fact, a follow-up study by Lazar's team found that after meditation training, changes in brain areas linked to mood and arousal were also linked to improvements in how participants said they felt – i.e., their psychological well-being. So, for anyone who says that activated blobs in the brain don't necessarily mean anything, our subjective experience – improved mood and well-being – does indeed seem to be shifted through meditation as well.

4. Just a Few Days of Training Improves Concentration and Attention

Having problems concentrating isn't just a kid thing – it affects millions of grown-ups as well, with an ADD diagnosis or not. Interestingly but not surprisingly, one of the central benefits of meditation is that it improves attention and concentration: One recent study found that just a couple of weeks of meditation training helped people's focus and memory during the verbal reasoning section of the GRE (Graduate Record Examination – an entrance test for graduates). In fact, the increase in score was equivalent to 16 percentile points, which is nothing to sneeze at. Since the strong focus of attention (on an object, idea, or activity) is one of the central aims of meditation, it's not so surprising that meditation should help people's cognitive skills on the job, too – but it's nice to have science confirm it. And everyone can use a little extra assistance on standardized tests.

5. Meditation Reduces Anxiety – and Social Anxiety

A lot of people start meditating for its benefits in stress reduction, and there's lots of good evidence to support this rationale. There's a whole newer sub-genre of meditation, mentioned earlier, called Mindfulness-Based Stress Reduction (MBSR), developed by Jon Kabat-Zinn at the University of Massachusetts' Center for Mindfulness (now available all over the country), that aims to reduce a person's stress level, physically and mentally. Studies have shown its benefits in reducing anxiety, _even years after_ the initial 8-week course. _Research_ has also shown that mindfulness meditation, in contrast to attending to the breath only, can reduce anxiety – and that these changes seem to be mediated through the brain regions associated with those self-referential ("me-centered") thoughts. Mindfulness meditation has also _been shown_ to help people with social anxiety disorder: a Stanford University team found that MBSR brought about changes in brain regions involved in attention, as well as relief from symptoms of social anxiety.

6. Meditation Can Help with Addiction

A growing number of _studies_ has shown that, given its effects on the self-control regions of the brain, meditation can be very effective in helping people recover from various types of addiction. One _study_, for example, pitted mindfulness training against the American Lung Association's freedom from smoking (FFS) program, and found that people who learned mindfulness were many times more likely to have quit smoking by the end of the training, and at 17 weeks follow-up, than those in the conventional treatment. This may be because meditation helps people "decouple" the state of craving from the act of smoking, so the one doesn't always have to lead to the other, but rather you fully experience and ride out the "wave" of craving, until it passes. Other research has found that mindfulness training, mindfulness-based cognitive therapy (MBCT), and _mindfulness-based relapse prevention_ (MBRP) can be helpful in treating other forms of addiction.

7. Short Meditation Breaks Can Help Kids in School

For developing brains, meditation has as much as or perhaps even more promise than it has for adults. There's been increasing _interest_ from educators and _researchers_ in bringing meditation and yoga to school kids, who are dealing with the usual stressors inside school, and oftentimes additional stress and trauma outside school. Some _schools_ have starting *implementing meditation into their daily schedules, and with good effect: One district in San Francisco started a twice daily meditation program in some of its high-risk schools – and saw suspensions decrease, and GPAs and attendance increase. Studies have confirmed the cognitive and emotional benefits of meditation for schoolchildren, but more work will probably need to be done before it gains more widespread acceptance.*

Worth a Try?

Meditation is not a panacea, but there's certainly a lot of evidence that it may do some good for those who practice it regularly. Everyone from Anderson Cooper and congressman Tim Ryan to companies like Google and Apple and Target are integrating meditation into their schedules. And its benefits seem to be felt after a relatively short amount of practice. Some researchers have cautioned that meditation can lead to ill effects under certain circumstances (known as the "dark night" phenomenon), but for most people – especially if you have a good teacher – meditation is beneficial, rather than harmful. It's certainly worth a shot: If you have a few minutes in the morning or evening (or both), rather than turning on your phone or going online, see what happens if you try quieting down your mind, or at least paying attention to your thoughts and letting them go without reacting to them. If the research is right, just a few minutes of meditation may make a big difference."

It is worth noting the huge amount of research and scientific evidence backing up the usefulness of meditation. Especially the statistics showing that it rivals antidepressants for depression and anxiety in its effectiveness and without the unwanted side-effects that the medication causes.

Effective Affirmations

Affirmations are statements spoken confidently about a perceived truth that you want to become a reality. Using positive affirmations changes our beliefs by helping us to rewire our brains into believing the stated concept. This is because our subconscious does not know the difference between perception and reality. Note how we cry at sad films even though they are not real. Changing our mind to think positive thoughts prompted by the positive affirmation will then impact on our actions and behaviours. It is always good practice to replace negative thought patterns with positive ones.

Verbalising positive affirmations empowers us with a deep sense of reassurance that our words will become our reality. We increase the level of vibration and the feel-good factor by expressing positive affirmations and we restructure our brains to think that manifestation of anything is possible. It is important that you dig deep and believe and feel the affirmations. Making positive affirmations if you don't believe them can understandably, cause stress!

Below are some tips for effective visualisations:

1. Identify the negative thought e.g. "I am not good enough"
2. Externalise it by writing it down on paper.
3. Identify the opposite of that thought e.g. "I am good enough"
4. Dispose of the negative thought by crossing it out on the paper, tearing it up or even burning it. This makes your rejection more forceful.
5. It is best to use the present tense because you are starting to feel these beliefs now (not at some vague future date) so begin with "I am…" (not "I will…").
6. It is also very important to affirm what you are doing in a positive way. Don't express the affirmation negatively (as in something you will not be doing).
7. Make affirmations for yourself only
8. Keep them as brief as you can
9. Be specific.
10. "Associate" yourself into the visualisation – see below.

"Association", (as was mentioned previously regarding "anchoring" and "visualisation") refers to a situation where you imagine that you are actively involved in the scene. "Disassociation" is the opposite and is a situation where you are looking in at the image or scene from the outside so that you are not involved in the mental picture you are viewing. Effective affirmations, just as effective visualisations, work better when you associate into the mental picture not only visually by imagining the picture but also by using all your senses – to feel, hear, taste and touch what you are affirming.

Thoughts influence our words which in turn influence our actions. Positively affirming our dreams and ambitions reassures us that our actions will translate into our manifesting these dreams and desires. Here are some examples below:

"I possess the qualities needed to be extremely successful."

"Happiness is a choice. I base my happiness on my own accomplishments and the blessings I've been given."
"I wake up today with strength in my heart and clarity in my mind."
"My life is just beginning."

Nelson Mandela famously retained his positive resolve despite being locked up in prison for twenty-seven years and acknowledged that he used the following affirmation to profound effect: "I am the captain of my own ship". He also used this to spur on the captain of the South African Springbok Rugby team to beat the All Blacks in a historic game to win the 1995 Rugby World Cup. This was a hugely significant and symbolic win that helped unite a South African nation fragmented by racial mistrust.

EXERCISE:

Say any of the affirmations in the examples above, if they apply to you as a start, and then create your own individual affirmations based on your personal needs and wishes. It is important to establish a profound communication with the universe, to really mean and feel these affirmations – so say them with conviction, in your own unique voice and make it happen in the real world. It is better to have your eyes closed so you will not be distracted when you are making your affirmations.

They can be affirmed daily each morning or at whatever time suits you.

What is an Anchor?

An "Anchor" is "a stimulus which triggers a specific physiological or emotional state of behaviour". It allows us to access desired feelings immediately, which we can utilise to help us achieve desired outcomes. Anchors can be involuntarily created such as in a song that may trigger memories and emotions of an event from our childhood. We often unconsciously react to the effects of anchors, but they can both empower or disempower us, motivate or demotivate us. Fortunately, we can now consciously help ourselves and others to create an empowering and motivating anchor. This has previously been referred to in Chapter 3 as it can be used for a "Pattern Interrupt" technique. I have included it again in this section purely for ease of reference.

Anchoring Technique as an Effective Tool

Anchoring has many other uses in relation to self-care, increasing our energy vibration and it is an easy, effective technique once mastered.

Situations where you would benefit from applying an Anchor

(1)   Accessing a *resourceful state* whenever you need a boost such as before a business meeting or an interview.

(2)   Creating a new response to an old (maybe even disempowering) situation. We can shift out of a negative *mood* to a positive emotional response.

(3)   Changing a negative *association* to a positive one. Seeing the good in a situation where in the past we have been focussing on the negative. Maybe getting redundancy is a good example of this. Devastated and taking it personally that you were let go, you are feeling very down. Alternatively, now you may have the financial lump sum to start out on your own. I think many Waterford Crystal workers who had huge talent and were made redundant did this and turned the whole experience and situation into a positive one. Anchoring can be used to assist in changing the negative association of the redundancy to a positive association (a new start), by regular use of the anchoring tool.

(4)   Moving from procrastination to *motivation.*

(5)   Empowering yourself to create a positive emotional state at any time to make you feel better and feel more in control to *overcome fear or overwhelm.*

(6)   Choosing a positive *emotional response rather than an automatic* response.

The 4 steps to Anchoring

This is another approach to "anchoring" as an alternative to the ITURN model mentioned previously. In this approach, the 4 steps to anchoring (can be referred to as acronym RACE) are:

(1)   **R**ecall a specific time when you had the emotion you wish to anchor. It may be when you were in a particularly calm and confident state. Imagine that time and that state.

(2) Ramp this state up using visualisation and associating into a colourful, fast moving, colourful movie where the intensity of the image is increasing. Provide a specific stimulus at the peak of the state (e.g. press thumb and index finger together tightly) and Anchor. See the diagram below.

(3) Change your current state (so this is a "pattern interrupt") from the fearful state to the calm and confident state you recalled at step 1.

(4) Evoke i.e. set off the anchor to test if it has worked. See can you recall this calm, confident state whenever you apply the pressure of pressing thumb and index finger together. The technique above must be practised several times, regularly within a 24-hour period before the anchor will be embedded in your subconscious. You will then be able to recall the desired state at will, whenever you need to access it.

The "RACE" and "ITURN" Anchoring Models:

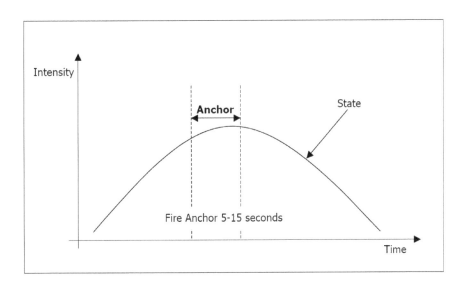

The "ITURN" Anchoring Model (that we looked at in Chapter 3) follows the same process as the "RACE" Model, but there is more of a focus on 5 key steps to successful anchoring. It essentially arrives at the same end-result as the "RACE" model. The 5 steps detailed in the "ITURN" model are reproduced below, again, for ease of reference.

1. The Intensity of the experience (of the desired state).

2. The Timing of the anchor. (Apply the stimulus at the peak of intensity).

3. The Uniqueness of the anchor. (It may be for one or several desired states).

4. The Replication of the stimulus.

5. The Number of times

For both the ITURN and RACE models to be truly effective, the practice must be repeated maybe even twenty times within a day to lock in this stimulus response pattern into your subconscious.

Motivation either "Towards" or "Away from"

Motivation can be a positive motivation "towards" a goal such as "to get fit by improving diet and daily exercise so I will feel and look better". This is a more effective mode of motivation than an "away from" motivation. "I need to lose seven pounds because I look awful and have a function coming up in a few months" is an example of an "away from" motivation.

The reason for this, is that the "away from" motivation arises from a need or fear of looking awful. As you start losing a few pounds, the motivation decreases. If you lose seven pounds for the function, then the goal is achieved so there is no further motivation. You will most likely resort to bad eating habits and fall into a yo-yo dieting pattern. This is a short-term resolution and consequently, the motivation is also short-term.

If you are motivated to feel good with no deadline, then as you start feeling good, you will want to continue in this positive frame of mind and body, so your motivation will still be there. You can usefully set target milestones for weight loss that can include a date for an upcoming function so long as that date is not the ultimate deadline. (Otherwise, your motivation will end because you have achieved only the short-term goal of looking good for that function). This "towards" motivation is not driven by a need or fear. It is for the long-term and sometimes is more of a positive lifestyle choice, so it is more effective and can be a part of your daily living pattern.

I have used diet and fitness as examples, but this approach to motivation applies to all aspects of life including fear of getting ill or fear of not earning enough money which are "away from" examples. Much better is the "towards" approach alternatively expressed as "I want to be healthy" rather than being afraid of being sick.

Similarly, being truly engaged and energised towards positive business goals with a focus on freedom and enjoyment (in addition to profitability) will yield superior results in business reflected in your income. Positivity attracts more manifestation than operating from a place of fear. For example, if you are focussed on just being able to make enough money to get by, then once you do have enough to get by, the motivation drops. How much more rewarding to earn more than "just enough" and to be able to enjoy the success personally and professionally. Additionally, you will be able to contribute not only to your own lifestyle but also to that of family and community.

If you observe examples within the business sector you will see that the most successful entrepreneurs are motivated by a "towards" mindset regarding their business goals. Consequently, they have much less stress and fear. This makes total sense when you think about it. They are energised, positively motivated and relish life's challenges which fits neatly alongside their achieving financial, personal and business success.

The Benefits of Practicing Gratitude and Writing a Daily Journal

A very useful tool for kick-starting the day into a positive and high energy mode is to take a few seconds when you wake up just to express gratitude – either just by thinking about it or, if this practice is new to you, then you can write it in your journal. Upon waking, we are in a relaxed and chilled, half-dreaming mood and are using lower frequency Alpha brainwaves. We can be more creative in this mindset, making it a good time for reflecting and journaling. We then move forward to our normal state and our daily routine using the higher frequency Beta brainwaves.

EXERCISE:

Start writing your daily journal. Choose an inspiring, colourful journal that you are attracted to visually or even the feel of it, if it has a bound, moleskin cover for example! Begin by expressing gratitude for five things. It could be anything such as your being healthy, your family being healthy, having a loving partner, children, pets or friends, having a secure home with adequate food and heat or some recent positive turn of events connected with your career, life or business. It sets you up for the day in a positive frame of mind. It is well worth it, and I do notice that my day is better when I stick to this approach.

By keeping an early morning journal to jot down what you have been dreaming about, can also indicate what is going on in your mind, be it good, bad or indifferent. The physical act of getting any negative thoughts down on to paper and out of your head is a release itself. They lose their power and can be dealt with more objectively. You can also jot down plans for the day, thoughts, ideas, visions (for vision boards) in fact, anything you like. You can also prioritise. This is an exercise purely to serve you, so it can be as detailed and structured or as simple and random as you want.

You can essentially therefore design a positive day ahead by crafting your dreams, vision, purpose and high-level priorities. Your thoughts and your beliefs are so important to the outcome of how you feel, to your ability to enjoy the day ahead and how open you are to manifestation. By offloading any negativity or issues on to the journal, they can be disassociated from your mind and dealt with objectively, in your own time thereby reducing overwhelm. You are in control.

Your mind, in the meantime, has also been freed up to accept positive thoughts, intentions and feelings for the upcoming day. This is a great self-care practice. Believe and trust in yourself that your goals in life, career and business are achievable. Know your value and your purpose. Your personal power truly does lie within you and all you need to do is to tap into it.

Sleep

Getting a good night's sleep is essential. Not only is it crucial to the regeneration of the whole organism but it is fundamental in fighting stress and high blood pressure. Experts recommend 7–9 hours sleep each night.

Lack of sleep can also cause depression, lack of concentration, poor work performance, accidents and impair effective communication with family, friends and colleagues. We intuitively know this, but we may not always act upon this knowledge. We would benefit greatly if we prioritise getting better quality sleep to rejuvenate ourselves and be better equipped to be fully engaged, alert and ready to enjoy our lives.

Make your bedroom a restful and peaceful environment. Avoid TVs, laptops, mobile phones or any electronic gadgets so that you can truly unplug and switch off. Keep it a work-free zone and an area you readily associate with sleep and relaxation.

Other tips are not to eat late, not to drink too much alcohol before going to bed (you may sleep but it will not be the same as a good, deep, restful sleep). Having said that, there is nothing more satisfying than enjoying a delicious meal and some wine with good friends to really reconnect and appreciate the good things in life. Forming a relaxing bedtime routine as you wind down is therapeutic and conducive to getting a good night's sleep. Relaxing in a bath with calming aromatherapy oils like chamomile, or one of my favourites, lavender, at the end of a day is an especially good way to unwind and helpful routine to prepare for a restful sleep. Candles and using aromatherapy oils in a diffuser also create a comforting and serene atmosphere as does listening to your favourite, calming music.

Snoring partners can seriously disrupt sleep, particularly if they lie on their backs. There are several throat sprays available based on the principle of toning and lubricating the soft tissues at the back of the throat to provide snoring relief – apparently – for up to eight hours. They do provide limited relief. Holistic remedies are also available.

The principle here of holistic remedies that I have looked at, is to tighten up the loose tissue in the throat that narrows the airway by stimulating the tissue to fill with blood. This plumps out the tissue and stops it sagging and vibrating which causes the noise. Two jars containing carrier oil, a sponge and essential oils; lavender in one, marjoram in the other are placed near the snorer. There is also the soothing impact of the oils relaxing us before we sleep. The lids can be replaced in the morning time. (This treatment should be kept away from pregnant women). Of course, it is important to follow the instructions on the tin for the treatment to work effectively.

Non-working Life

For some people, the most important thing in their life is their job, career or business and I was that soldier for several years. However, that does not mean that it should always be this way and you may want to shift to another lifestyle, as I and many others have done. I have certainly shifted my own perspective on life radically in the last few years. Perhaps what is needed is to merely to simplify your life and reduce your stress levels so that you are spending more time doing what really matters to you. This can be achieved by just reducing the number of working hours. A simpler lifestyle can bring greater freedom to do what you really want to do (which may lead to another career or even starting up your own business). You can have more freedom for the other things in life that bring you more satisfaction and joy.

In most senior roles, reducing your hours (in my experience) is not feasible. I will never forget as a young (and only female) accountant managing a team in an extremely macho environment, being told by one person that he would never have hired me as I would just get pregnant. Charm was not his strong point. I am sure that worse has happened to many young, working women but I understood the message. I made sure I was self-employed when I had both of my children and postponed doing so until I felt secure enough both financially and professionally. This attracted huge criticism from all sorts of (unexpected) sources. Tough. It was a good decision and I still believe that and apologise to no one.

Giving birth is one of the truly amazing miracles anyone can experience. It should never be compromised. I received no maternity benefit from the state in those days (being self-employed) but nor did I want it. I had decided that my values were not the same as Ireland at that time and that I could earn enough money and more importantly, wanted enough space, to have my children at my ease. After having my daughter Colleen, I took a year out because aside from wanting to love and care for her and be with her, I genuinely could not entrust such a vulnerable little baby to anyone's care if I had even the smallest reservation about them. Second time around with my son Shane, I had learned so much more and trusted my instincts more confidently. Guess what – work came to me in the form of name your hours and price (within reason, obviously), whenever you are ready. I returned to do some work with a company who sold, implemented and troubleshot Financial software and who had experience of my work on several of their sites over the years. Consequently, three months after Shane was born, I worked four mornings a week whilst Colleen was in the naionra (Irish speaking pre-school) in the nearby village of Rathcoole. That way, I was able to spend time with both children whilst doing a regular four hours a day for four days a week. However, I still returned to my negative embedded belief that I had to keep working long hours within less than a year, so I am not gloating by any means.

Holidays are an invaluable part of the ability to unplug from technology and to de-stress. Taking a break from your work when you finish each day, at weekends and on vacation is essential. The break gives you a chance to pursue interests outside of work and to enjoy rest and recreation with your family, friends and pets. Not only will this boost your spirits, but it reminds you that you have an identity outside of the working environment. It is a mistake to bind your interests, friendships and relationships to the work environment only. I am not preaching here as I have been guilty at one stage of all the above.

Equally, it is a mistake to value yourself by the amount of work that you do. If your self-respect is determined by your work accomplishments, you will never be able to exit the so-called, enchanted circle and you will never manage to work less. Everyone is expendable in the work environment even though sometimes there can be a subtle carrot and stick approach to lure you into feeling that you are crucial to the organisation. Recognising that everyone is expendable is an important realisation.

Hobbies, especially creative ones, such as music or painting, volunteering and sports that you find challenging and engaging, allow you to "turn off" and are a healthy release. Creativity with children, romance and friendship are equally, if not more important, facets of life. Realistically, most people need to work to earn money and it helps if you enjoy your work. It should always be placed in context, however, in order that you enjoy a happier and more rounded lifestyle.

In summary, regularly disconnecting from work and from technology in the evenings, weekends and holidays is a necessity in recharging your batteries and concentrating fully on enjoying quality time for yourself, friends and family.

There is a lot of wisdom in the phrase "Working to live not living to work".

Chapter 5

Time Management and Overwhelm Strategies

What is Overwhelm?

Overwhelm is a state when we have so many simultaneous priorities to get done that all the numerous thought patterns about each individual job or project start to run together in a disordered fashion. The subconscious becomes overwhelmed and confused as it is under tremendous pressure and cannot sort the thoughts out. The resulting behaviour is frozen, a "cannot think straight" scenario. This state can last for several days or even weeks.

Managing Overwhelm and Practical Exercises

Firstly, before doing anything, take a few deep breaths to calm yourself down. The most effective breaths are very deep breaths called "Buddha Breaths" and are physically better for your body. You breathe in deeply so that your stomach extends as the air fills deep into your lungs (rather than in shallow breathing in which you raise your shoulders up and down). As you exhale slowly, your lungs empty and deflate, so your stomach returns to normal. Not pretty but it works. When you are inhaling, try to do this for five seconds and when exhaling, try to extend the length of the breath to seven seconds. This type of breathing will lower your heart rate, your blood pressure and the stress hormone cortisol so that the overall impact is to calm you down.

If necessary, imagine that you are taking yourself way out of your body and visualise looking down from above the earth. The problems will appear miniscule in the grand scheme of things. When you do come back down, in a calmer state, you can use the following technique, tailoring it as needed for yourself.

The following is just one of many practical strategies to manage overwhelm. It is an amalgam of many ideas from many sources so tailor it to suit your purposes.

EXERCISE:

1. Write down everything you should do on a piece of paper. A master list if you like. Divide it into the different areas of your life. If it helps, you can use a highlighter to colour code each area. Resist the urge to use technology for this task. Somehow writing on paper (and then the physical act of crossing things out) creates momentum. You are also "disassociating" from the tasks and have put them on paper so that your conscious mind can make sense of how best to execute them. You also clear your head by getting them outside of your head and down on paper clearing space so that you can think more clearly.

2. Delegate if appropriate, especially in a work situation where some of these tasks may not really be your responsibility. Consider if you do them merely because you are used to doing them or even just like doing them.

3. Spend 15 minutes approximately, knocking out as many of the easiest, fastest tasks as you can. Make your quick phone calls. Send your short emails. Don't worry about whether these are the most important tasks on your list. You're moving forward. The goal is to cross off as many items as possible in the shortest time. Use a timer, if that helps, to keep you focused. Batch similar tasks together so that you are not doubling up on work.

4. When the 15 minutes are up, turn off your phone, close all the windows or tabs on your computer, then prioritise.

5. Choose the most daunting thing on your high priority list, the one that instils the most stress or is the highest priority. Then work on it and only it, without hesitation or distraction, for example for 35 minutes or whatever is more suitable, if it warrants less time.

6. After 35 minutes, take a break for 10 minutes and then start the hour-long process over again, beginning with the 15 minutes of quick actions.

7. Learn how to say "no" politely, so that the list is not unnecessarily expanding, unless it is something genuinely important and urgent: "I'll come back to you, but right now, I have an extremely full schedule" might be a useful example in a work situation.

By adopting the above (or similar) framework, you will be making progress and executing and finalising many of the tasks that previously caused the overwhelm. By taking actions in a methodical manner, you are back in control.

Time Management

To be organised externally in life or at work, you first need to organise yourself internally by defining your priorities, values, goals and how you personally want to organise your work and life.

At work, you will define what you need, what to do and when to do it so as to perform the tasks assigned to you in your job description and to contribute to your team effectively and efficiently. By doing this, you will avoid unnecessary, stressful work situations. Often one hour of planning can save many hours of execution. Start with defining what your desired outcome or goals are, to get clarity on what must be done to achieve them.

Below is an interesting and useful article by Jon Mathews, Don Debolt and Deb Percival on Time Management that may give you some ideas. They raise some critical issues. It is written with entrepreneurs in mind, but it raises helpful pointers for everyone.

"How to Manage Time with 10 Tips That Work

Chances are good that, at some time in your life, you've taken a time management class, read about it in books, and tried to use an electronic or paper-based day planner to organise, prioritise and schedule your day. "Why, with this knowledge and these gadgets," you may ask, "do I still feel like I can't get everything done I need to?"

The answer is simple. Everything you ever learned about managing time is a complete waste of time because it doesn't work.

Before you can even begin to manage time, you must learn what time is. A dictionary defines time as "the point or period at which things occur". Put simply, time is when stuff happens.

There are two types of time: clock time and real time. In clock time, there are 60 seconds in a minute, 60 minutes in an hour, 24 hours in a day and 365 days in a year. All time passes equally. When someone turns 50, they are exactly 50 years old, no more or no less.

In real time, all time is relative. Time flies or drags depending on what you're doing. Two hours at the department of motor vehicles can feel like 12 years. And yet our 12-year-old children seem to have grown up in only two hours.

Which time describes the world in which you really live, real time or clock time?

The reason time **management** gadgets and systems don't work is that these systems are designed to manage clock time. Clock time is irrelevant. You don't live in or even have access to clock time. You live in real time, a world in which all time flies when you are having fun or drags when you are doing your taxes.

The good news is that real time is mental. It exists between your ears. You create it. Anything you create, you can manage. It's time to remove any self-sabotage or self-limitation you have around "not having enough time", or today not being "the right time" to start a business or manage your current business properly.

There are only three ways to spend time: thoughts, conversations and actions. Regardless of the type of business you own, your work will be composed of those three items.

As an entrepreneur, you may be frequently interrupted or pulled in different directions. While you cannot eliminate interruptions, you do get a say on how much time you will spend on them and how much time you will spend on the thoughts, conversations and actions that will lead you to success.

Practise the following techniques to become the master of your own time:

1. Carry a schedule and record all your thoughts, conversations and activities for a week. This will help you understand how much you can get done during a day and where your precious moments are going. You'll see how much time is spent producing results and how much time is wasted on unproductive thoughts, conversations and actions.
2. Any activity or conversation that's important to your success should have a time assigned to it. To-do lists get longer and longer to the point where they're unworkable. Appointment books work. Schedule appointments with yourself and create time blocks for high-priority thoughts, conversations and actions. Schedule when they will begin and end. Have the discipline to keep these appointments.

3. Plan to spend at least 50 per cent of your time engaged in the thoughts, activities and conversations that produce most of your results.
4. Schedule time for interruptions. Plan time to be pulled away from what you're doing. Take, for instance, the concept of having "office hours". Isn't "office hours" another way of saying "planned interruptions"?
5. Take the first 30 minutes of every day to plan your day. Don't start your day until you complete your time plan. The most valuable time of your day is the time you schedule to schedule time.
6. Take 5 minutes before every call and task to decide what result you want to attain. This will help you know what success looks like before you start. And it will also slow time down. Take 5 minutes after each call and activity to determine whether your desired result was achieved. If not, what was missing? How do you put what's missing in your next call or activity?
7. Put up a "Do not disturb" sign when you absolutely must get work done.
8. Practise not answering the phone just because it's ringing and e-mails just because they show up. Disconnect instant messaging. Don't instantly give people your attention unless it's crucial in your business to offer an immediate human response. Instead, schedule a time to answer email and return phone calls.
9. Block out other distractions like Facebook and other forms of social media unless you use these tools to generate business.
10. Remember that it's impossible to get everything done. Also, remember that odds are good that 20 per cent of your thoughts, conversations and activities produce 80 per cent of your results."

The above article describes a practical approach and depending on the complexity of the work and the amount of staff that you are managing, it may form the basis of your own time management strategy. In most office work places, Excel Spreadsheets are commonly used for listing and scheduling tasks and action plans. Therefore, I think Excel is a tool worth mentioning in any time management discussion. "Clock time" is more important for paid employees than for entrepreneurs as employees do not have as much freedom to decide how they will work and their time is often dictated by the tasks their managers have scheduled for them.

Effective To-Do Lists and Scheduling

The article raises some interesting points and is quite useful in that we should challenge our approach to managing our time, if we are struggling in this area.

When I do my daily journaling, my journal is part gratitude, part ideas, part plans (including the day's priorities) and part observations. Whatever works for you is good. The journal is a broad-brush approach that I have more leisure to do now that I have changed my lifestyle and exited the formal finance world.

In that formal finance world, the work was very much task-driven, and I always used "To-Do" lists. Examples could be calls that need to be made, necessary meetings, scheduled tasks such as financial reports with commentary, answering e-mails, reviewing work of staff directly reporting into me, project planning, tax deadlines, preparing financial reports and statements. I say in the "formal" finance world as I am still involved with Finance albeit in a reduced manner. There is still an important role for thinking and prioritising aside from executing tasks however. This can get even quicker results.

Forward planning, as alluded to previously, is always much better than a knee-jerk reaction to problematic situations. Most of these situations could have been avoided had they been planned more carefully. Fire-fighting decisions can often be compared to short-term sticking plasters. To resolve issues conclusively often requires more thought and in-depth planning so that the solution is a longer-term one. It is much better to plan positively beforehand and therefore avoid the problem situations that can result otherwise.

I have encountered a few managers throughout my career who hop from one thing to another and never really work effectively. In doing so, they constantly interrupt and prevent their staff (and sometimes colleagues) from working effectively too. I truly believe that all managers require training and that just because you have been in an organisation for a relatively longer time than others, that this does not qualify or equip you to deal effectively with staff. Management and supervision of staff is a whole new area of expertise that requires different skill-sets rather than just being good at your previous job. As we know, most people who leave, do so because of their managers' lack of management skills rather than a dislike for the organisations themselves.

Always consider alternative viewpoints to yours however, especially if you feel uncomfortable about them. Dig deep down to see why you are feeling this way, as it is quite possible that this discomfort is prompted by there being a kernel of truth in what the other person is saying. It may be that you are unwilling to acknowledge this. Perhaps you can learn from this other viewpoint. Your manager may have a broader understanding of the impact of performing tasks a certain way. If you are technically weak in a certain area, then ask for training. It can be informal training just as much as it can be formal. You can always proactively learn about new areas yourself.

Scheduling is another tool that enables you to make best use of your time and resources to achieve stated goals or targets. By not only planning for the routine tasks but very importantly, factoring in contingency time for unscheduled events, you will increase the chances of a successful outcome. Scheduling assists in breaking down the tasks and steps in various processes and thereby forces a realistic and more detailed understanding of the nature of the processes themselves. This will produce a feeling of being more in control, especially as you can conduct regular reviews (with your team also) and make necessary tweaks. All of this enables a quicker response to changes as they crop up. Thereby reducing the risk of unforeseen issues arising that can scupper the plan. As this is a much more controlled approach, there is a certain level of confidence among the team regarding a successful outcome.

A feeling of greater control and a detailed consideration of contingencies (with built-in resolutions should these situations happen) produces not just more confidence in the project outcome but importantly, it lowers the general stress of the entire team. Nobody enjoys, nor do any companies benefit, from ill-thought-out plans that have people flailing from one catastrophe to another and constantly being on edge. This firefighting type of approach also tends to lead to excessive overtime, high stress levels, unnecessary errors, staff absenteeism and quite often staff burnout. Factors influencing how people use scheduling include their own work situation and the level of responsibility they have within the organisation, their current life structure, industry sector, available budget and personal tastes.

A commonly used approach can be a weekly 5-step process, as follows:

1. Identify the *time available* for personal and work goals.
2. Schedule in all *essential tasks* that cannot be delegated or avoided.
3. Schedule in all *high priority activities*.
4. Schedule *contingency time* in for unexpected events.
5. The *discretionary time* available that is now left can be used to review priorities and goals.

Scheduling tools include diaries, calendars, organisers, integrated software such as Materials Requirements Planning (MRP) on Oracle for instance (for scheduling material demand), stand-alone software scheduling packages such as MS Outlook and MS Project.

Tools such as Microsoft (MS) Outlook can effectively schedule tasks to do, meetings, deadlines or whatever is important to you, into your calendar and you can then decide upon their priority. It is not necessary to attend every meeting you are invited to. It is important to be selective and ensure that the meetings are properly run with clear agendas. Minutes should always be recorded and will include the effective Action Plans that have been agreed upon at the meeting. To keep the momentum going, the minutes should be distributed as soon as possible after the meeting to all involved parties. Momentum will be maintained if this is done within a few hours of the meeting.

Effective Meetings and Action Plans

The agenda should be distributed to all meeting participants preferably at least a day before the meeting. This will give the meeting participants time to think and prepare for the items to be discussed. Although there may be some important additional items that arise during the meeting, they should only be discussed at this meeting if they are relevant to the Agenda. If the situation warrants it, another meeting can always be arranged for a later date to revisit any important items that are not strictly relevant to the original meeting, but which require follow-up actions.

Effective Action Plans should include a brief description of the item, the action to be taken, by whom and by when. The person chairing the meeting must ensure that the meeting stays on track and guide it back when someone starts making irrelevant speeches or goes off-topic. It's also an excellent idea to highlight the deadlines for completing actions, to indicate their priority and if any other resources are needed. The person who will arrange for these additional resources to be provided and the timeline should also be specified. Resources can include training as well as equipment, hardware, software and additional staff or engaging outside expertise.

Meetings can be the greatest time-waster ever. Never let your valuable time be wasted. Instead, value your time and focus on the relevant tasks relating to your work and only attend relevant and effective meetings that get results and that do not over-run. There may be meetings to highlight changes in the company regarding restructuring, objectives or system changes etc. so these will obviously be relevant also. You will quickly learn which meetings are important and which meetings to avoid.

"Not-To-Do" Lists and Setting Boundaries

It is not unheard of (in work and at home) to be assigned or expected to do tasks that are not actually your responsibility. This can cause conflict as well as the stress of overload. It may appear to be easier sometimes to just keep motoring on as you always have. However, this is a short-term view and the situation will not only never improve if you take no action, but the behaviour will become even more entrenched. This step of identifying responsibility needs to be addressed before it gets to the stage where it is assumed that you are tacitly agreeing to accepting this additional responsibility.

You can take note of the above on your own, private "not-to-do" list, then request a meeting with your manager or even your family and discuss the tasks that are causing the problems in a calm, rational, dispassionate and objective way. There could be all sorts of reasons for the misunderstanding so don't indulge in negative self-talk and feel that there is a conspiracy against you. Generally, the cause of the misunderstanding is down to bad communication.

Once the items are objectively assessed in a logical and objective manner and the communication is crystal clear to everyone impacted, then if appropriate, certain tasks can be reassigned to others or even back to the person who should have been originally responsible.

Examples of items on a "not-to-do" list include items that are assigned on another person's job description that you are regularly doing, unless of course, you are officially covering for them if they are on vacation, for example. Another example is doing work that is outside of your own and your department's remit even if you enjoy doing it, perhaps just because you enjoy tinkering with IT problems. This type of activity should be minimised. It is beneficial to be aware of the workings of the IT systems business in general, but your focus should be on your own specific responsibilities and tasks. Critically review the tasks that you are currently doing, be it at home or at work. Identify the areas that you do not have to do, so that others (especially in a domestic situation) can share the burden. You can also refuse, in a tactful way, to constantly make yourself available to anyone and everyone. The ability to say "no" is essential to moving forward in your work and life in general.

Other areas to consider include not volunteering for every committee, project and community initiative that pops up. It is not effective to always be available and is much better to block off time in your diary when you are unavailable. This can be used for your own personal "thinking" space and for planning. It is always counter-productive to get in the habit of reacting to situations rather than proactively planning your day ahead.

Delegating at work is an extremely important skill for managers as it challenges, stretches and develops less experienced employees in addition to freeing up the manager's time to do tasks that the more junior employees cannot do or that are too important to delegate. Not delegating (be it at work or in the home), is a major source of overwhelm. You cannot do everything – so plan, prioritise and delegate as appropriate. In many cases in a work situation, there are several low-level tasks that can and should be automated within the IT systems. Proactive proposals to automate and streamline such processes to free up your own and your team's time to do the higher added-value work is to be encouraged. To do this you must first understand the IT systems.

Understanding your company's IT system is an invaluable way for you to do your work more efficiently and to spot logical and justifiable opportunities to streamline processes. This streamlining can result in avoiding duplication of effort, eliminating unnecessary work and improving the quality, timeliness and usefulness of for example, Monthly Management Reporting Packs. Preparing and running unnecessary reports that were once of use but have now been superseded by newer ones is a common example of a waste of time and effort. Always keep an open, enquiring mind when viewing what you are doing versus what your objective is. There is usually scope for improvement in the way work is currently being performed. There are always opportunities to improve upon IT processes. However, if you don't understand the basics of the IT systems, you will not be open to availing of these opportunities.

Constantly checking e-mails is just as time-wasting as going to every meeting that you are invited to. Ensure that you are benefitting and receiving value from the activities that you are investing your precious time in. In a Global organisation, where you may be involved in several world regions, it is unrealistic to accept invites to every meeting for each country and then the subregions, especially with the time differences between for example the US, Europe and India. Then consider the different working days in the Middle East (weekend being Friday and Saturday, so Sunday is a working day). If there is an expectation that you should be working in this manner, then look at the possibilities of delegating or consider whether it is a healthy work culture. Maybe it does not serve you to work in such a culture?

If your obligations at work are unrealistically large and you perceive that there are other problems with the company's culture, thoroughly analyse the situation first before taking any decisions. It is preferable to present a suggestion or solution when you approach your manager so that you have at least a starting point for a discussion, rather than just merely presenting with problems for others to sort out. Your manager will be under pressure too and will appreciate a more proactive and helpful approach from you to resolve the situation.

We can all identify the people who only present with problems, blocks, excuses and this negativity causes them to be an energy drain on everyone. Negative behaviour lowers morale within a team and generally reduces productivity. Office politics is also another huge problem. Many people are promoted not because of merit but for political reasons. They may also be quite astute at presenting themselves and their contribution in a more favourable light. You can possibly learn from this. If the company culture does not align with your own values, then it may be time to consider leaving.

Be far-sighted and realistic. If you want to work less in the same company and this can be accommodated, go for it, but clearly understand that you may well be paid less. If necessary, switch roles within your existing company or even find a new job. Be prepared for this change and remember that generally, it is easier to find new employment if you are still in employment. Maybe this is even a good time for you to start your own business?

Microsoft (MS) Project Software

This, as the name suggests, is extremely useful for projects both within the workplace and within your personal life, as it is more sophisticated than a simple excel list that only takes into consideration the tasks to be done. With MS Project, you can factor in the necessary sequence, specific timings and the necessary inter-dependencies regarding the various tasks within the project. Contingency plans should always be factored in, as inevitably things may not go to plan for any number of unforeseen, internal or external reasons. I have used MS Project on small projects and on larger, two-year projects as a Consultant when sourcing, implementing and training staff on new hardware and software packages. Following on from this, by trouble-shooting any teething problems, ensuring the integrity of the financial information produced. Finally, compiling user-training manuals and training staff on the new systems. MS Project was hugely useful in scheduling and executing all the tasks involved and was used for sub-projects too.

You can also use MS Project within the personal arena, as I have done when we were building our home and using it for planning a disparate variety of projects and tasks. I am going into more detail regarding this and the objective is not to bore you ! I want to illustrate how useful MS Project can be in very different scenarios outside of the work environment. There were in fact five projects when we were building our home.

The first project related to the initial land purchase, obtaining planning permission (including my presenting a Business Plan to Kildare County Council for an organic smallholding) and finalising the architect's plans.

The second project was the construction of the house and garages. The milestones of constructing the house from site excavation, sinking a well, groundworks, blockwork, plumbing and electrics, plastering, painting to the purchasing and installing internal fixtures, fittings and furnishings can all be included on your project plan. Tasks and timelines with the necessary sequencing of those tasks and inter-dependencies are easily and clearly mapped out using this tool. Obviously, as my husband works in construction he was very familiar with the various construction stages but to coordinate the project was important too, especially as I was pregnant at the time.

The third project related to the setting up of my commercial Organic Strawberry business. Having produced my business plan and it being accepted by Kildare County Council (which was vital to our getting the planning permission in the first place), I then needed to obtain an organic grower's license. There are three Organic certification bodies in Ireland and I chose the Organic Trust.

The tasks in this project related to ensuring the treatment of the land conformed to the rules and regulations in the Organic Trust Handbook. I followed all the procedures regarding record keeping and passing organic audits. My degree came in useful as did the huge amount of research I had carried out in the year prior to purchasing the land. This research centred around:

- Strawberry varieties
- Spanish style polytunnels (that could be vented to allow free movement of air to minimise occurrence of the mould botrytis)
- Installing tee-tape irrigation systems with mipex, valves and timer
- Gaining experience working on an organic farm in Wicklow (albeit they did not grow berries but great practical experience nonetheless)
- Totally understanding the rules and regulations as laid down by the Organic Trust handbook
- Sourcing customers (Tesco were my first and their strawberry spec was two pages long!)

These were all considerations to be incorporated into the project plan and all had to conform to the regulations in the Organic Trust handbook. They did. This was before I even grew any organic strawberries, the regulations regarding growing produce are also detailed in the Organic Trust handbook.

Application for grants for organic farming under the Rural Environmental Protection Scheme (REPS) was also another important area to be factored into the project with attendant duties, responsibilities and submissions to Teagasc and the Department of Agriculture. Especially as farming when certified organically, attracted twice the grant! Money aside, I have always been very environmentally aware and truly believe that being in nature and enjoying all that it brings to us, is vital to our wellbeing. I had originally wanted to study Landscape Architecture as opposed to becoming an accountant. That was why I decided upon doing an essentially ecological degree (Botany and Physical Geography) at Durham University. One of the main reasons I was attracted to studying Botany in Durham was the pleasure of attending lectures, seminars and practicals under the tutelage of Dr. David Bellamy, one of my heroes. The Geography faculty in Durham was also one the best in the UK at that time. In fact, it still is. I studied Physical Geography, so studied soil science and ecology. This, together with the Botany side of my degree, came in very useful for growing the organic strawberries.

The fourth Project was the construction of the service building (to check, weigh, pack and store the strawberries). I applied and received a capital grant for this (eventually, but only because Tesco, a British Multinational sent a letter to the Irish Department of Agriculture to say they would buy my produce – ironic?!) MS Project allows you to plot when key milestones in the project should be achieved. I am not getting sponsorship from MS or from Tesco by the way!

The fifth, smaller project, related to producing a Landscape Layout and Programme, as requested by Kildare County Council, prior to obtaining planning permission. I had originally wanted to be a Landscape Architect and now I had free rein on our very own land! Out came the cartography pens from my student days in Durham and it was truly a labour of love. Obviously not a professional job but you can also do this too. The Plan was fully executed aside from planting the leguminous crops in the field. I am giving you sight of the detailed programme and the land use plan. Again, this is not to bore you but to make everyone aware of your own potential and that you too can do this.

An elderly and good friend of mine and ex-neighbour when we lived in Newcastle in County Dublin, had remarked to me at the time when I was explaining my plans to him, "Jaysus Mary, you will be long dead and gone before all those trees grow". Well, delighted to say, they have all grown and I am still alive! He did love the taste of the organic strawberries too so that was encouraging as he was a very plain and honest speaker!

DETAILED PROGRAMME FOR PROPOSED LANDSCAPING

LANDSCAPE FEATURE	SCHEDULED DATE
1. Site Entrance (as per Condition 7 & 10)	August '96

2. House and garage construction
   * In accordance with drawings submitted
     - as per Condition 1
   * Blue Black Slates
     - as per Condition 5
   * External Finish of uniform, neutral colour
     as per Condition 6
   * Biocycle Waste Water Treatment
     - as per Condition 8
   * Well, biocycle and percolation areas
     - as per Condition 9
	October '96

3. Beech hedge at entrance & around Bungalow	October '96
4. Alder Hedge	October '96
5. Hawthorne/Ash hedge	October '96

6. Alternate Beech and Ash trees to
be planted in existing Hawthorne/
Ash hedge bordering road.
   * Retaining existing hedge & trees
     - as per Condition 10
	October '96

7. Polytunnels:
 	
   Polytunnel 1
   Polytunnel 2
   Polytunnel 3
	
	February '97
	February '98
	February '99

8. Lawn area	March '97
9. Grassland and Leguminous area	March '97

11·5 ACRES - KILTEEL, CO. KILDARE

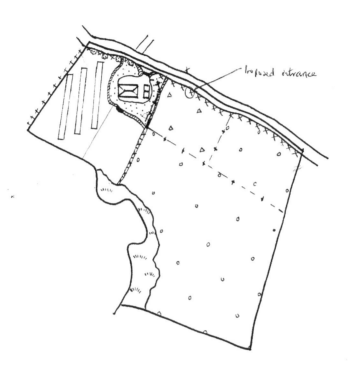

Proposed entrance

KEY :

O.S. Sheet Kildare 20/2

Scale 1 : 2500

⊠ x x x x	Existing Hawthorne (some ash) hedge
x|x|x|x	Proposed Hawthorne (some ash) hedge
+ + + +	Proposed Alder hedge
▨	Proposed Beech hedge
☐	Proposed Polytunnels (max no.= 3)
❀ ❀ ❀	Proposed Ash + Beech trees (alternate) ie to shield Polytunnels.
+─+─+	Grass Track

Crate (3 in all)

Proposed Lawn

Proposed Leguminous Crops

Proposed Grassland

145

Time-wasters

Time-wasters are another reason why we are less productive, miss deadlines and then feel stressed and overwhelmed. Firstly, you need to identify what your own specific time-wasters are and then eliminate or minimise them. The following extract is taken from an article by Natalie Gahrmann (an American coach and author) and is an excellent summary.

In item 8 of her article, I would also add in "social media" as it can be very easy to become distracted by socialising too much online. Whilst social media is necessary in a lot of instances for marketing purposes, it can waste time if not controlled properly. Limits should be set on the number of times that email, Facebook, LinkedIn, Twitter and Instagram are checked daily. If using social media is critical to your job in marketing and advertising campaigns, obviously you will spend more time working on this genre.

EXERCISE:

Read the following article and see how you can benefit from taking note of the advice and tips offered.

"Timewasters by Natalie Gahrmann.

Time is a very precious resource. The fact is that regardless of how well you manage time, at the end of a day, you will still only have had 24 hours. In one year, there are still only 8,760 hours. The key is using your time efficiently and eliminating time wasters from your day. Your attitudes and behaviours affect how you use your time. Below are some examples of ineffective use of time. By substituting what's not working for you with a more effective behaviour and/or attitude you're on the road to managing your time.

1. INTERRUPTIONS/DISTRACTIONS
If you have a constant stream of well-intentioned colleagues, subordinates and/or family members interrupting your concentration and focus, stop them by communicating when it's okay to interrupt and when it's clearly not.

2. POOR PLANNING.
Planning is so critical when you want to accomplish something. Planning provides direction before proceeding toward a goal.

3. PERFECTIONISM

Although perfectionism is a behaviour it's also an attitude. By striving toward progress rather than perfection, you will free up a lot of your time and energy.

4. PROCRASTINATION

Like perfectionism, procrastination also is both a behaviour and an attitude. Waiting until the last minute or otherwise putting things off tends to create a crisis or problems that may not otherwise exist. In addition, by not doing something you're procrastinating about, you also end up wasting too much time worrying about how much you're procrastinating. Just do it.

5. TRYING TO DO EVERYTHING YOURSELF

Taking on the world all by yourself will not serve you or the people around you. Learn to say "no" and to delegate tasks others can do for you (even if it's not up to your standards).

6. TAKING ON TOO MUCH.

Biting off more than you can chew is a prime example of taking on too much. Not having strong clearly communicated boundaries is another example. You do not need to volunteer to be on every project, organisation, taskforce, association, etc. It is useful to appreciate that even though you cannot control other people's attempts to encroach upon you (be it entering uninvited into your own personal space or crossing a boundary in a work situation e.g. delegating work to you inappropriately) you can control your own response to this. So, you do retain your power and in realising this, you will not feel powerless.

7. CRISIS MANAGEMENT

A crisis is an unforeseen emergency. By planning and asking yourself whether something is truly urgent, what will happen if it's not handled immediately, you will eliminate a great deal of this fire-fighting behaviour. Remember the adage, "haste makes waste".

8. TOO MUCH SOCIALISING

Although we all love to have friends and enjoy our relationships, by allowing yourself too much freedom in this area you'll wind up spending a sizable percentage of your 'work' time socialising and will be pressing to meet deadlines.

9. NOT VALUING YOUR OWN TIME.

Others will not respect or value your time if you don't. Send the message that your time is important. Watch your actions, behaviours and commitments – are they communicating the right message?

10. LACK OF SKILLS

Organising, prioritising, decision-making and problem-solving skills are all critical in supporting effective use of time. Strengthen these skills and you'll see a remarkable difference in how you use your time."

The suggestions above can also be used as a starting point for discussion by HR professionals within their own companies or in wellness seminars run by Life and Business Coaches. It would not only be useful to enable staff to make better use of their time but may also give pointers as to how the company might assist them should any persistent problems come to light.

There are many strategies and tools that can be used to manage our time more efficiently and to manage and prevent overwhelm. It is worth HR Departments and Management generally, to address this area and thereby minimise all the associated problems subsequently caused to staff health, morale, productivity and to the business generally when this is not done. I hope some of the ideas, tools and tips discussed in this chapter are useful in this regard.

Chapter 6

Understanding and embracing Corporate Life

Changing your Attitude about Money

Do you have conflicting attitudes towards money? We all appreciate the benefits that money can bring. Equally, we are aware of the hardships, compromises and conflicts that exist when money is scarce. Much as we can appreciate the advantages of having money and wealth, there can often be an unease or conflict around possessing or being seen to possess, a large amount of wealth. If you are a people-pleaser then you may be content to have "just enough" rather than risk annoying others who have less. Wealth can also attract begrudgery from others who resent your success.

Values and beliefs influence behaviour and there can exist a commonly held belief that even discussing money (or to be heard discussing money), is vulgar, distasteful and greedy. This results in a lack of objective dialogue around this whole area by many people, despite the critical importance of money in our lives. It is better to remove the embarrassment and awkwardness around your attitude towards money if this is a negative self-limiting belief that you hold. Everyone, at some level, knows that money is necessary, not just to survive, but also to enable a better quality of lifestyle. Honesty around money is a much healthier attitude to hold.

Some people do manage to live high quality lifestyles with very little money but generally these are people who maybe own their own houses and/or can grow their own food. For the most part, however, people living and working in large towns and cities have more demands on their finances such as rent, mortgages and the need to buy all their food. Making and managing money is a critical area therefore.

Examples of direct results of holding negative beliefs around money, can be an awkwardness around billing clients, under-quoting for work or even not asking for a well-deserved pay rise. In many cases people can be reluctant to ask for overdue payments from their customers or clients. This is obviously not good for business. It is not good for anyone on a personal level either as if you are struggling to identify your worth to others, it can indicate that you don't really place enough value (including monetary value) on yourself. Your self-esteem and confidence will undoubtedly be lowered by such negative thinking and the resulting behaviour it produces. You will also attract more of the same lower vibration back, if you do not grasp this reality. There are enough people out there who can sense a chink in the self-confidence armour and will take advantage of you, so you owe it to yourself to be financially savvy.

Stating what you are worth regarding your wealth and the services you provide does not sit easily with many people, particularly women. Below is an exercise that everyone should do.

EXERCISE:

Write down what you believe you are worth financially – have a good think first and back it up as if you are making a business case. This is because you **are** making a business case – for yourself. It is worth doing this even if you feel extremely uncomfortable about it. List and value your assets and then look at what income you receive for your work versus what you believe your services are worth. We will come back to the results later.

As an accountant, I have never had a problem quoting corporate clients either market or above market rates (based on my track record and results). Similarly, I had no problem asking for a rise when in employment or for a better package in interview situations. This is partly due to my values and beliefs but also the more success a person has achieved, then their reputation and self-esteem naturally grows and the easier it gets. However, I have been guilty of not being objective in other situations where there were favours being asked of me, in a personal capacity, outside of my normal working day job or career.

I had been approached by several people (outside of my work environment) who needed my accountancy or taxation skills but who basically wanted this accounting or tax work done for very little or in a couple of situations, for nothing. Quite often, they were starting out in business, in trouble or even crisis, imminently due in the High Court or having been issued notices by the Sheriff regarding seizing their assets for non-payment of taxes. It could just have been as simple as their lateness in arranging for their accounts to be prepared. As a result, there was late filing and their taxes were not being paid on time. Naturally, such situations are preventable and unnecessary but still required speedy resolution. That was where I came in.

I have helped people in the situations mentioned above – gladly and with no reservation. In other instances, preparing accounts, tax returns or by dealing with third parties such as banks, solicitors and Revenue on their behalf. However, when a few of those people were blatantly playing on my good nature (plus being very manipulative in doing so), I no longer accommodated them. This type of situation is not healthy for anyone involved. The result for me was that I was working for very little and at times that did not suit me (late at night). On one occasion, I was presented (after the tax deadline had passed) with incomplete bank statements in the middle of my daughter's fifth birthday party?! It was time to call a halt. The recipients of my services in these cases, still thought of themselves as deserving immediate attention and still needed to learn the life lesson that everyone should accept responsibility for their own actions and inactions and the consequent repercussions. It is important that everyone takes responsibility and be accountable for their behaviours especially when that behaviour leads to "crises" of their own making. As grown adults, nobody should expect to be "bailed out".

From a personal growth viewpoint, remaining stuck in a world where others are expected to take on your responsibilities of your tax being paid on time, for example, yet the information presented to prepare the accounts was always late and incomplete, was disrespectful towards me and not very clever business-wise for the "client". The other downside is the undesirable situation if a tax deadline is missed, then late interest and penalties will be incurred, negative attention from the Revenue will result and being the subject of a court case or of their assets potentially being seized by the Sheriff quite clearly can follow. Fortunately, these clients were in a tiny minority and I no longer deal with them.

Basically, if a professional service is provided, clients should expect to pay for this service at the going rate. In my own case, I then had to sit back, start taking notice of both behaviours (mine as well as theirs) and reassess the entire situation. By being objective and business-like about the scenarios above, I realised that I had to change my own behaviour. The life lesson I learned was that whilst some people may never change their behaviour, I can always change my reaction towards it. I subsequently explained when faced with any similar situations again that I was too busy and recommended that they try someone else. In most cases, this was true but that is to miss the point. The lack of respect for my time and the lack of value that was placed on me amounted to disrespecting me both in a personal and professional capacity. Seriously, why would you or I go there? I didn't normally and have now finally learned that I will *never* do it again. I will always charge what I and the value of the service that I am offering, is worth.

Emotional blackmail by friends, family or by relatives (connected by blood or marriage) is effective on a very short-term basis only.

Women, particularly, have an additional expectation placed upon them that they should always please people. This expectation has been conditioned into their subconscious by family, religion and society in general. It is important for us to appreciate this fact and to be able to critically analyse if this thinking has any validity. It may suit others for women to accept this belief, but does it serve us? Women therefore must also stand back and objectively assess this to see if it logically stacks up. It is totally appropriate to say "no" in many situations, be those situations to do with family, work, personal relationships or in society generally. It can be about doing excessive (unpaid) overtime at work (both men and women alike), being taken for granted in a relationship or merely because the other person "felt entitled". If you are in such a situation be it your manager at work, your partner, children, friends or even with family or in-law connections, the message is just the same. I suggest you say, in the words of another QTT Practitioner, "That doesn't work for me", or words to that effect. In a more formal work situation, it may be that you say you will get back to them as currently you are working on whatever project or task that it is. If it is still urgent, then suggest that they try someone else. That way you are being spared negative backlash but have made your point in an assertive manner without flatly refusing.

Initially, it may be difficult to adopt this mindset, but you will gain more respect from everyone if you not only value yourself, but you are also seen to be placing value on yourself. In the longer term you will have more satisfaction and self-esteem because not being valued causes discomfort and stress. I know that it did in my own case.

Another important learning is that by viewing your time as less valuable than it is, you are sending out a message to everyone in your life that you and your contribution, be it at home or work (both in self-employed or in an employee role) is not worth that much. In this situation both you personally and your expertise or professionalism will continue to be disrespected in the future. You need to own your role in allowing this negative situation to persist. When you do appreciate yourself and take a stand, then this more positive acknowledgement and appreciation of your own worth will be reflected in your vibrating at a higher energy frequency and you will benefit from the knock-on effects of abundant manifestation. You will attract the right clients who will pay you accordingly.

Clients, friends, partners, family, in-laws or employers who try and undervalue you regarding your time or by not paying what you are rightfully due is a common issue. It can often be resolved by simply changing your own behaviour towards them and the situations that are presented to you. Changing your own behaviour and asserting yourself positively is the best way to progress in your career, business and personal life. Taking back your power in situations where you were previously disempowered is the way to go. It is never too late for us to learn from these experiences and to change the way we react to such situations.

Women in many sectors are still being paid less than men and this trend is changing but in general, the change is very slow. One reason why it is not changing even faster is that women tend, generally, not to be as assertive as men in making a business case for themselves. It is vitally important that we, as women, understand this, own it, learn from it and act upon it.

How can we Improve our Relationship with Money?

A better way to look at money is to view it as **objectively** as possible and face the reality that you not only need it for the basic demands of food and shelter but also for many other enjoyable things in life. This can include your own personal development by further study, hobbies, maybe start a family, progress in your career or purchase cars and holidays. If you are quite ignorant about managing your finances – why not do a finance or accounting course purely for yourself? This will take the mystique and fear out of the whole area of finance. The knowledge will also assist you in planning your finances effectively and efficiently so ensuring that necessary bills and taxes get paid on time and your savings and pensions can start accumulating. You will also feel much better within yourself knowing that you are more in control and confident around money. The fear will have gone.

EXERCISE:

Assess (for a second time) what you should realistically be getting paid at work and state the case for this on paper in an objective manner. This means cutting out any drama or seeing yourself as a victim or somehow being uniquely deserving due to having several children, a perceived lack of opportunity to change or whatever excuses you have been telling yourself over the years. You are what you are, so perhaps now it is time to move on, get over yourself and focus on your positives. It will be so beneficial to your own self-esteem and growth when you do this. In doing this second, personal business case, consider the following:

- What the market is paying (get salary surveys, Google competitor business etc.) for similar people in your current role. This can also be done using the larger recruitment agencies' reports on remuneration packages in the various industry sectors. If you are self-employed and provide a service, you can google and research market rates.

- Realistically assess how you stack up regarding other fellow employees in the same role in your organisation? Often there are formal pay rate scales for each job title reflecting the level of work that you are doing. There is normally an upper and lower financial range of pay within which the employee at that level can be paid. As it is a range, then there will be an element of discretion (usually with input from your direct manager) regarding whether you are placed more towards the upper or lower end of the scale. Take this into consideration going forward.

- List what other value you are adding to your job or to the services that you provide. Take the "personal" out of it and make a cold, clinical and objective assessment. Do you volunteer for any projects? Are you a proactive problem-solver? Do you have several services (rather than one) that you provide e.g. reiki, coaching, QTT practitioner, yoga, reflexology etc.?

- What academic but arguably, more importantly, technical or professional qualifications do you have. Are you progressing by gaining such qualifications? This will make you more valuable both to the business (or your own business) if you stay and to you personally if you decide to leave and go out into the marketplace for another role.

- Have you gained particularly useful experience, either previously or within the current company by taking on and successfully completing new or more complex projects? Have you had notable successes in your coaching career? Are you writing a book? Have you done any public speaking?

- Are you available to provide back-up when your manager is on holiday and step out into and be willing to learn about more senior areas of work?

- Do you come up with proactive ideas and solutions to problems or ways in which to improve any aspect of the business and its processes? This is preferable to merely presenting with problems that you expect others to solve. Be clear and objective about your financial value to the business.

- If the business case stands up for you to earn or charge more, then this is logically what you should do. Nothing less.

We need to be able to confidently ask for what we are worth. Compare what your results are regarding "what you are worth" after considering the above with the results of the earlier exercise at the beginning of this chapter. Is there a difference? Is the second exercise more accurate?

Request an annual appraisal if you are an employee, if this is not already done. You can then see how your manager assesses how you are performing. One of the most useful aspects of a performance review is to identify the areas where you can improve your performance. Do not take the appraisal personally as it can provide you with constructive criticism to help you to improve. Always ask about opportunities within the company to help you to improve the areas that have been identified as those where you are most challenged. This could be in the form of internal or external training, an opportunity to work on other projects, gaining experience within other areas of the organisation or being sponsored by the company to pursue professional qualifications. There is a debate regarding the usefulness of an annual performance review, suggesting that feedback should be an ongoing dialogue instead of an annual event. It is obviously preferable if feedback is an ongoing conversation but until a better alternative is working in practice, I do not see anything wrong with having an annual review. An annual review does provide you with some objective evidence regarding potential pay increases and promotions.

Superior performance reviews warrant good pay increases and bonuses. Austerity measures were introduced during recessionary times and resulted in pay cuts and reductions in other benefits. However, these recessions are cyclical events, so they do not last forever. Equally, by making positive contributions in your work, demonstrating a positive and proactive approach in both team and individual scenarios, you will be growing and achieving a reputation as being a professional who achieves results.

Depending on the roles you apply for, I recommend that you ask about additional benefits particularly in supervisory or managerial roles. Commissions should always be included in remuneration packages for roles in sales as an additional impetus to achieving and even surpassing sales targets. Bonus schemes are common as are share option schemes. Do not shirk from realising that if you don't ask and if you don't appreciate your own self-worth, then others will be only too pleased to offer you less.

If you appear happy to settle for this, then they too will be more than happy! Even though larger organisations have guidelines on pay structures, it does not necessarily mean that you should automatically start at the lower end of the salary scale for your specific grade. Qualifications, experience and successful results that you have obtained or contributed to should also be considered when making the decision. You owe it to yourself to make any such relevant information available and present it in an objective fashion. You are making an effective business case for yourself.

It often amazed me looking at the wages, salaries and bonus schemes in many of the companies (but not all) that I have worked in. It was very interesting how the male versus female remuneration packages stacked up, especially knowing what contribution some of the individuals really made. You need to appreciate your worth, using past achievements, qualifications and relevant experience to make the best case possible in an objective and assured manner, as I keep stressing. It's not being greedy, vulgar or unfeminine; it's business and more importantly, it's **your** business. Contrast this with the general attitude of men who even though they sometimes may be less qualified, less capable and less hardworking, do not have these same qualms. Learn from it!

Embrace and Enjoy the Challenge and Journey in Corporate Life

If you have chosen to work in a corporate environment, then it is important to realise that there are several advantages as well as disadvantages, depending upon the specific "corporate culture" that you are operating within. I have worked for European Multinationals (MNCs) and US MNCs in permanent roles and as a Consultant. I have found that the culture in the US MNCs has a much more challenging, if not sometimes unreasonable, attitude regarding a person's holiday entitlements. This is for many reasons.

In Europe, we are accustomed to at least 20 days holidays, in addition to public holidays, however, this is not the case in the US. See an extract from an article "Paid Holiday Schedule" by Susan Heathfield, below:

"Susan M. Heathfield
Updated November 26, 2016

Paid holidays are not required in the United States by any government regulations. This is because the Fair Labor Standards Act (FLSA) does not require an employer to pay employees for time that they do not work, such as for vacations or holidays.

Paid Holiday Averages in the United States
Employees in the US receive an average of <u>7.6 paid holidays,</u> according to The Bureau of Labor Statistics in the category "all <u>full-time employees</u>." Professional and technical employees average 8.5 paid holidays.

Clerical and sales employees average 7.7 paid holidays. Blue collar and service employees have, on average, 7.0 paid holidays.

A 2016 <u>study of paid time off</u> by the World at Work Association found that 9 paid holidays was the norm in the United States."

This article helps to explain the differing attitude towards holiday entitlements in US MNCs to those in European MNCs. In one US MNC I worked in, almost everyone in Finance was required to work Bank Holidays because the Irish Bank Holiday Mondays all tended to fall on month-ends that year. This may appear to increase productivity for the MNC, but it also reduced staff morale to a huge extent. High staff turnover reflects this dissatisfaction and that is very costly for any company.

Excessive (and unpaid) overtime is also expected at senior level in many organisations. This may be more acceptable if you are at the start of your career, are ambitious to learn, achieve and be promoted. It is less attractive when you have been doing it for decades, have other family commitments and are being pulled in several directions resulting in becoming stressed out, eventually sick and possibly even depressed or burnt out.

The time difference between the US and Ireland is also another reason for longer hours than in an equivalent Irish company. I found in some US MNCs that there tended to be (too) many meetings and that this meant that several of the US meetings did not start until 5pm or 6pm in the evening Irish time/GMT. This is clearly the time when the Irish working day would ordinarily be coming to an end.

If dealing with different global regions such as the Middle East, another factor to be considered is that their weekend is Friday and Saturday so that their working week includes Sunday. Additionally, they are not available on Friday. This also means sometimes having to be available on Sunday and being aware of the need to work around the fact that there is no office presence on Fridays.

Laptops can provide flexibility for work both during (if travelling) and outside of working hours. However, this facility can be a double-edged sword as it can mean that it may be expected that you are virtually always available for on-line meetings, emails and compiling reports as examples. Basically, this results in your working outside normal office hours on a routine basis. You are in effect, constantly available receiving emails at all hours of the day and night. The "out-of-office" feature does not deter people copying you in on countless emails, irrespective of whether you are in work or not. Similarly, this applies to Blackberries and iPhones.

The obvious thing to do is to decide a cut-off point for switching off from technology and then stick to this rule. Depending upon the corporate culture if others, in your team and your manager are full on 24/7, there is often an unspoken expectation that you do the same especially if you are in a senior position. At this stage, even though I was previously guilty of not doing it, I firmly believe that it is essential that when you leave work each evening, weekend and on holiday that you "unplug" from work.

Having said all the above, the senior roles in MNCs tend to pay well with good salaries and have packages that include other benefits (that you should always enquire about) such as:

- Company pension scheme (what rate does the company contribute – as this will be no cost and will be tax free for you). You will get income tax relief at standard rate (20% at September 2018) on the personal pension contributions that you make.
- Private health and dental care (for you and possibly family members).
- Death-In-Service Benefit (where the employer pays out to your next of kin if you die whilst in the employment of the company). This can be quite generous and four times the final salary is quite common. This is a form of life assurance.
- Share Options.
- Company car (or payment-in-lieu instead).
- Educational assistance for course costs with paid study leave days.
- Professional Subscriptions such as ACCA, ACA annual fees.
- Employee Assistance Schemes – where you can access a third-party company that will provide free legal advice, counselling advice and other advice about work or personal issues.
- Bonuses.
- Profit-Sharing Schemes.
- Mobile phone.
- Laptop.

- Using health and leisure facilities provided by the company or if external, paid for by the company.
- Company Credit Card and expense accounts generally.
- Travel. I always used to try and take an extra day or two to explore a new European city and relax after the work was completed e.g. stay on for the weekend.
- Ongoing Continuing Professional Development Training (CPD) as required by certain Professional bodies such as accountants, pharmacists or architects. This can be provided in-house or by external trainers.
- Subscriptions for organisations linked to your area of expertise.
- Subscriptions to golf clubs or other clubs where business can be done or generated.
- Staff discount on the products or services that the corporation offers.
- Subsidised canteens.
- Company loans.
- Ask about any other perquisites/perks.(Google organise a dry-cleaning service for their staff!)

The above perks were obviously trimmed substantially during the recent Irish recession but undoubtedly, as the economy improves, some if not all will once again be available.

Depending upon the corporate culture, you can gain a wealth of experience on the business sector itself, different IT systems, processes and best business practices. Knowledge of communicating and working with and in other countries, regions, cultures and interacting with your colleagues in those countries, is a separate and enjoyable learning experience of itself. Learning other languages can also add to this experience.

The International aspect to your experience provides you with an additional useful and marketable skill to the basic tasks and duties that you are hired to perform. I found working in and visiting offices in other parts of Europe and forming friendships with colleagues from diverse cultures to be a particularly satisfying part of working with an MNC. There is a huge sense of achievement when you face up to and overcome the additional challenges when engaging upon International assignments. It is extremely beneficial for personal and professional growth. International assignments are a long-recognised way of developing potential senior managers in many large corporations. All of this is good for your CV.

You can also earn a lot of money! To summarise, as with everything there are pros and cons that you should weigh up. If you do decide to go the corporate route, then the following sections can offer you some very constructive and practical advice.

Using the Company's Internet and Intranet Sites

Undoubtedly, you will have visited the corporate website when doing research for your interview in the first place. However, once you are employed you should still become more familiar with both the internet (available to the public) and the intranet (available to employees of the corporation only). There is a wealth of information to be obtained regarding the history, evolution, strategy, goals, products, services, current hot topics to name but a few, in relation to the corporation and business activities. My first port of call is always the financials. I look at the investor page on the company website to see the details of the financial results to see how the corporation is performing. This was especially useful when several companies had cash and liquidity problems during the recent economic downturn. Liquidity is important i.e. referring to how easily a company's assets, such as stock, can be converted to cash in the event of a cash shortfall. This gives an indication of how well the corporation will cope in times of austerity. If there are healthy cash reserves, then this can be an advantage for a potential employee in choosing that company to work in. It will give the potential employee, additional security that the company will not fold.

It is also always good to know how profitable the corporation is as well as how healthy its cash flow position is, before signing up. This will often determine the level and quality of the remuneration package available. Importantly, it can be a good indication of the engagement and general morale of the workforce. However, even if the remuneration is good, if the working environment is fraught, unhappy with low energy and a disassociated workforce, then you will most likely not enjoy working there. Most people have probably worked in organisations that had very bad staff morale and the only reason for staying there was to fulfil their financial obligations. Longer term, it is better to find a more satisfying alternative employment. If you spend most of your time at work, then this is a big consideration. Continual stress can affect your energy and your physical, mental and emotional health. I deal with stress and its management in Chapter 7.

Unfortunately, many manufacturing MNCs that had been doing well prior to the recent recession in Ireland, pulled out when times became tough. Alcoa (renamed to Kawneer), GE Security and WYG were a few I worked for that were affected. They exited Ireland during the downturn or significantly down-sized in the case of WYG. In Alcoa and GE, I was Financial Controller and was then appointed to Finance Director. In WYG my role was on a contract as a Change Manager and Interim Financial Controller. That role was during a period when WYG were winding down operations in Ireland, making engineers redundant weekly and closing country-wide offices. Safe to say that morale was not great but then that was symptomatic of a lot of workplaces at the time. Everyone was impacted when the recession hit but there are lots of lessons to be learned from those challenging times. Redundancy money can often be used by the newly-redundant ex-employees to kick-start small and medium-sized enterprises. Or even to take some well needed time out to recharge your batteries.

Other interesting, useful facts and news can be obtained on the intranet that the public will not be privy too. You will get indications of what direction the corporation appears to be moving towards. New research and development demonstrate the focus they are following for new products, services or markets and most importantly for you, new opportunities. Many positions will be advertised internally and if you want to relocate you will be able to see suitable positions in the location of your choice. In this respect, there is huge opportunity in Global MNCs and you can register your interest and be in the front line when a suitable position in a suitable location arises. It is looked very favourably upon by MNCs, in terms of promotion, if you have worked on an international assignment as previously mentioned. It is also a huge opportunity to experience a different culture and lifestyle whilst still having the security net of retaining your permanent, pensionable job.

Another useful area of information on the intranet is to see who is being promoted to what position. Whilst it is a good plan to avoid negative, petty office politics, it is important to be aware of the "big picture" and to see who the senior management figures are and to be aware of the major changes, restructurings, acquisitions and disposals. This overview, together with the day-to-day operational view of your own role gives you a much more complete understanding of the business and how you fit in currently and where you could go in the future. When being interviewed for a new role internally, this type of awareness shows a real interest and an aptitude to move from local to European, or even global level roles. Aside from which, it can paint quite an interesting picture!

As you progress in your career, make sure you update your LinkedIn profile and invite colleagues and managers to be your connections. Building up an online profile is hugely useful. I have obtained work via LinkedIn so don't overlook its potential usefulness. When you are preparing for an upcoming interview, look up your interviewers to see their backgrounds, interests and if you have anything in common regarding people, companies or business sectors. It all helps to create rapport. Now that I have changed my focus to Life and Business Coaching, I expect that many more of my clients will come from LinkedIn and Facebook.

Familiarise Yourself with the Chart of Organisation

A Chart of Organisation should be available on the intranet. It will show Senior Executives and possibly Senior Management roles and lines of reporting. In companies that are involved in a start-up situation, there may be a lot of fluidity at first as the dynamics can be very fast-moving as the structure develops. New people are continually being sourced, transferred and new posts are being created. The HR Department should be able to provide a local, Irish Chart of Organisation for you as should your direct manager. I always asked for this when embarking on a new role, irrespective of whether it was a permanent role or a consultancy contract. I personally, have had an unpleasant experience in one work situation where an accurate chart of organisation was not in place and my own role was unclear to others. This is a huge mistake and can cause unnecessary confusion, stress and conflict. The chapter of my life where I worked in corporate is now completed but I still emphasise the need to ensure clear and accurate communication regarding people's roles. Not to do so is unfair to everyone involved and wastes a lot of time and feeds internal office politics in a negative way.

It is important to know who does what and who to go to, if necessary, for certain information. In the financial world which I experienced, for instance, it was necessary to know the contact person for tax information, financial, investment or IT for the different European regions. As organisations grow, the functions are outsourced, and this can be stressful too due to the different time zones. Updating standard costs on IT systems the weekend prior to the 1st January when you are liaising with India and the US over the New Year weekend can be a pain. Eventually it was successfully executed but was unnecessarily stressful and as the process was done each year, I was unsure as to why it was not more seamless and fluid especially in a very large Corporation. It should not have involved the hours that I worked over that New Year weekend. Sometimes big is not necessarily best.

It is also helpful for you to see how you and your department slot into the overall organisation so that you gain better understanding and can work more effectively within your direct team. You can then more fully appreciate the interaction of both yourself and your team with other teams and departments. By doing this you can be a more effective and enlightened contributor. You can also see where there are vacancies or scope for promotion, should you wish to change roles.

Know and Understand Corporate Policies and Procedures

Every business especially larger corporations have (or should have) policies and procedures in place. Where there are gaps, you may even be involved in writing up the outstanding policies and procedures using the relevant corporate format used for their existing policies and procedures. Familiarise yourself with these to understand how to correctly execute your designated tasks. However, always be alert to the fact that nothing is set in stone and that there is always scope for improving and streamlining them as changes occur in business, IT, work practices and as new legal or corporate demands arise.

There are always differences between MNCs due to different IT systems, the diverse types of business and in some cases a different corporate cultural emphasis. Even though there is a prescribed way to treat fixed assets for example, in the financial statements of a company, the process of getting there may differ from the previous corporate you worked for. Therefore, you will need to be familiar with your current company's policies and procedures. How you get to the compliant result may be very different and you need to understand this and not cause any non-compliance issues with internal or external auditors. The same principle applies to any department be it sales, production, inventory, finance, quality, procurement, human resources and health and safety being the main ones.

Being familiar with the policies and procedures will enable you to perform your role with more confidence, knowledge and speed. Naturally, this will always be appreciated by other team members and by your manager. This increased knowledge and efficiency should result in freeing up more of your time. As part of your own personal development and to allow you to develop your skills, experience and confidence, your manager may then ask you to assist with other tasks or projects. This is a sign that you are progressing as you have mastered your previously assigned tasks. It is also an opportunity for you to learn and grow. Embrace this challenge.

However, if you are constantly struggling to complete the original tasks that you were assigned, then there is less chance of this realistically happening.

Importance of Job Description, Understanding Goals and Personal Development Plans

Hopefully, when you started your new role, Human Resources (possibly with some input from your own department) engaged you in an induction course. This would take the form of a general overview of the actual physical premises, health and safety information, general HR Procedures regarding holiday applications, time sheets, office hours and followed up with a company handbook for employees. The induction course can be in-house or in the case of GE, my induction was held in Gdansk in Poland with other recently appointed GE staff from various parts of the globe and from different disciplines such as sales, engineering, HR.

These induction courses will give you the space and time to gain an overall appreciation of the corporation's goals, ethics, values, history and possibly, an outline of their strategic plans. Importantly, it will be giving you an insight into the specific corporate culture of the organisation that you have just joined. It is good advice to familiarise yourself with the corporate culture before you even apply for a job. If you are not a good fit with the corporate culture, it may save you a lot of frustration by simply not applying. Look towards an organisation that has similar values to you as this will make everything so much easier in the long run.

You should have already familiarised yourself with your job description as part of the preparation for your initial job interview. It is quite possible that the basic job description will be followed up with a more detailed breakdown of your assigned tasks once you have completed your induction course. For example, a detailed monthly checklist with designated tasks (sometimes even at designated times) on designated days assigned to various members of your team for the month-end close would be common enough in the finance world. It is important to ensure that not only are you familiar with your job description (ask for clarification of anything that you are unsure about) but also any other scheduled tasks that support the overall duties on your job description. If you have a handover period or have access to the person who previously performed your role, then this will be an even more effective way for you to transition into your new role. The best approach is to see how much you understand and then maybe organise a short meeting with your predecessor at a mutually convenient time, rather than an ad-hoc approach and peppering them with a multitude of questions at what may be an inconvenient time for them. If they are leaving the organisation, then they can possibly have more time with you to handover the role.

The IT systems may or may not be familiar to you. Quite often, there will be online training available for you or in-house training may be arranged. Ensure you are aware of when such training is being held and that you sign up and attend, if necessary. Ensuring that you gain access to the various IT systems is also important. You do not want to find out that you cannot for example access certain reports or functions that you need for month-end, when you are under pressure to meet a month-end deadline. Generally, you should have the same access permissions as your predecessor, unless your job description has been expanded or changed. It is always worth finding these things out beforehand. Problems on IT systems in MNCs normally require you to log an issue, so take note of the case reference number and follow up if not resolved in a timely manner.

There is always a learning curve in any new position even if you are familiar with the general nature of the tasks that you are expected to perform. Different IT systems and procedures for doing the same generic tasks exist in different organisations so be prepared for this and be open to learning and be flexible to change. Nothing is ever set in stone.

Know and Understand Your Manager's Goals – Manage Up

Corporate/MNCs will have performance management processes for all their staff in place. Although you will not be expected to set out goals and personal development plans immediately upon joining, after a certain period (for example after a probationary period of maybe six months) this will then be expected of you.

In my own experience, the goal setting process varies widely within MNCs. Your Manager may suggest the more critical areas that they are concerned with in guiding you to formulate goals in those areas. Generally, the optimal approach is that the employee comes up with their own SMART goals (as discussed in Chapter 1) which can then be discussed and reviewed with the line manager. If you own the goal, there is a much greater chance of success than if someone is micromanaging you and telling you what your goals are. Your own input and ownership of your goals is vital to your success in achieving them.

At the same time, if someone is setting their own goals, they should be relevant and aligned to that of the team, their manager and to the corporate goals. If your manager does not indicate their goals to you (and if corporate goals are not available on the intranet), then I would ask. A good, experienced manager should be aware of this but as with everything in life, managers come in all shapes, sizes and quality!

I mentioned previously in Chapter 1, the benefits of having a personal goal that aligns with a corporate goal. I used an example of learning Spanish as a personal goal and getting sponsorship from your employer to do this if you can make a business case for it. If you can arrange that the personal and corporate goals are aligned, then there is a double benefit or synergy making the goal even more compelling.

Finally, it is useful to realise that sometimes you may have to manage your manager or "manage up". There may be times when you are being asked to do tasks which are of no benefit for the business and are effectively a waste of your time. Before expressing anything about this, thorough evaluation of the nature of the task, time spent, and the value gained need to be carefully examined. For example, running reports or preparing schedules, that were historically useful but that no one now uses is a common one. In the past, the reports or schedules may once have been critical, however, that information may now be available in newer, updated reports, rendering the older reports unnecessary. Doing a monthly journal with 5,000+ lines is another example where employees were expected to work blindly without performing any critical analysis of the reason for performing the task. Gather the facts and present a business case to your manager and suggest that you could spend time on other more value-added work rather than continuing the same work, just "because it was always done". Be prepared for the resistant manager who may prefer to maintain the status quo either because of a lack of awareness and knowledge or else, a fear of change. It may be that it is perceived that to change would involve a time commitment and they just cannot appreciate the bigger picture and the long-term benefit. Try and present a logical business case and suggest a more effective alternative. Unfortunately, this can happen a lot but don't allow it to cloud your own judgement and set you back. Continually strive to improve processes and performance and to reduce unnecessary tasks where there is truly no benefit or value to be gained.

In other cases, it may just happen that there is a good reason (that you are unaware of) for running for example, a report. Ask so that you can understand as you should always try to improve and streamline your work processes. Aim to be working smarter rather than just harder. If as a last resort, you are getting nowhere, then it could be time to look elsewhere for a job.

Another area regarding "managing up" is the ability to politely say "no", to a request that is outside your area of responsibility. It may be that you say, "I cannot do that as I have task a, b and c to complete first", especially if these are key to your role. If you require some training on a new area you could express interest and request training. I have touched upon this area in the Time Management section in Chapter 5.

Always be aware if you are on a bonus scheme of the exact way in which the bonus is calculated. There is little merit in neglecting the tasks specified in your job description and on which you will be evaluated when your bonus is calculated. Continually spending excessive time on doing tasks that essentially someone else is responsible for, is not a smart way to work. If this is a continuing issue, it is best to clarify the matter with the person responsible in a tactful manner and if all else fails, ask to meet with your line manager, in a positive, objective and business-like way. Also, show willing if you are interested in taking on more work. You will always need to be flexible but also to be able to assert yourself in situations such as this.

In general, it is best not to approach your manager with "problems". Try to resolve the issue yourself first and if unsuccessful, have a few positive, pro-active solutions or proposals available. This makes perfect sense if you think about it. At least, when you have analysed and really examined the situation, you are in a better position to contribute positively to an optimal solution, even if you do not know what this might be. Collaboration with your manager and team is always preferable to conflict.

Be Professional – Dress, Punctuality, Language, Behaviour, Rapport.

Punctuality is important for your professional credibility at work. If you are a consistently poor time-keeper, miss meetings and important phone calls, take longer breaks than you should and take noticeable time out "sick", you will be perceived as being unreliable and unprofessional. This will result in your being someone in the team who causes unnecessary work for others. Quite understandably, you will be passed over when new opportunities arise. A manager will not pick someone who is going to let them down and in turn make them and the team, look bad.

This also applies to the way you dress. "Dress for the job you want, not necessarily the job that you have," is sound advice. First impressions are powerful and creating a professional visual image is a huge plus. Naturally, it needs to be followed up by using professional language, positive, can-do attitude and behaviour, as well as the ability to execute your job. If the corporate dress is casual, take care that you never let it become too casual.

One area that frequently lets people down is the area of office politics. Avoid gossiping and negative behaviour. You can be aware of what is happening, but it is best to do your work, be helpful, positive and proactive but not to join the "nay-sayers" and cliques that exist in every office to a greater or lesser degree. Politics is a part of human life, but small-minded, negative behaviours are the bane of any company and prove problematic for the manager to manage, causing other team members to feel ill-at ease. This is not conducive towards enabling a positive, happy and productive workforce. It is also symptomatic of a low-level vibration and so will attract similar. Have you ever noticed how morale in a workforce once tainted by negative vibes/vibrations can so quickly spiral downwards? Ideally, aim for high energy vibration and excelling at your work, enjoying it, progressing and learning new things and above all, being positive and professional. This is a good strategy for you and for your contribution towards your work and when progressing throughout your career.

The next section on "Rapport" is linked to the ideas above. Even though we are all intuitively aware of rapport, it is worth examining deeper.

How to gain Rapport

Rapport is when we positively connect with another person or people, be they colleagues, direct reports or people that we report into; in fact, with anyone we interact with in our personal or professional life. It can improve your communication with colleagues, your team, your managers and your interpersonal communications with anyone. Below I am giving you the theory behind some of the NLP techniques to gain rapport.

Rapport is based on the concept that when people are like each other, they also like each other. Considering the other person's needs and not just their own needs is central to this approach. There are definite ways of building and strengthening rapport. These include how we construct our language, how we use body language and how we amplify language and phrasing. Studies indicate that words account for only seven per cent of communication, tonality accounts for thirty-eight per cent and physiology fifty-five per cent. NLP teaches various techniques to build rapport.

Mirroring and Matching are two NLP techniques used to build rapport using body language rather than words.

Mirroring is when you copy the movements of the other person so that your behaviour mirrors theirs, much like a reflection in the mirror. Mirroring can occur naturally when rapport does exist, or it can be done purposely to create or increase rapport. It is often used deliberately within sales and life coaching but clearly must be done in an authentic way. It is not appropriate to abuse this or to be too obvious in any work or personal situation. My own view is that it is far preferable that mirroring occurs naturally and that the knowledge about mirroring is used as an indicator to check that rapport exists. Its existence is a very useful guide to confirm if rapport exists within teams. People in rapport within a group will often mirror each other's behaviour naturally.

More tellingly, it can also be a useful guide indicating where rapport does not exist between members of a team. This can therefore flag a problem that needs to be resolved.

An example of mirroring is when you are naturally in rapport with someone, you subconsciously put your left hand under your chin when speaking to them and they may be doing the same thing with their right hand.

"Matching" is another useful technique to check if rapport exists.

Matching is when you match the movement of another person. An extreme example being if the client raises their right arm, you also raise your right arm. Matching, as with mirroring, happens naturally when people have rapport between them. An example of good rapport within a group using matching as an indicator is when everyone has, their right legs crossing over their left knees.

Other examples where matching can occur are:

(1) **Matching the Internal Representational System** of the other person. See Chapter 1 where Internal Representational Systems are more fully explored and explained. To recap, the Internal Representation can be predominantly visual, auditory, kinaesthetic or auditory digital. You can match the way in which the other person experiences the world. They may experience the world mainly by what they see (visual), hear (auditory), feel (kinaesthetic) or understand (auditory digital). You will be able to communicate in the most effective and efficient way possible with the other person by understanding how they best experience the world. You can connect with them using the same type of language that they use. "I see what you mean" or "describe the bigger picture" are two examples of the language that a predominantly visual person would use. I am repeating this explanation of internal representational systems here for the benefit of people who are dipping in and out of the book. (I have done this frequently within the book for the very same reason so bear with me!)

(2) **Matching the physiology** of the person you are communicating with by for instance matching hand movements, posture, facial expression, eye blinking rate or movements. Such matching undeniably sends a message to their subconscious mind that we like and are liked by them. Again, this observation of matching physiology occurring naturally is very useful for checking if rapport exists with the person or within group situations. Leaning in towards each other would also suggest rapport.

(3) **Matching your voice** is another example. Rapport can be gained by noticing and deliberately altering your own voice tone, volume and tempo so that it matches the other person. This can help to diffuse situations where there are heightened emotions and a person may be agitated. Lowering the voice tone, volume and tempo signals a less aggressive stance and may calm the individual concerned.

(4) **Matching breathing** is yet another useful and empathetic example. Sensitively matching breathing so that you also breathe at the same rate, from the same location (high, middle, low), not in an awkward or blatant way. By adopting a soothing and encouraging manner you can also create more empathy as well as rapport.

(5) **Matching the manner that the other person processes information and speaks** creates rapport. This also applies to the size of pieces of information they use. Do they perceive the bigger picture or are they more into specific details?

(6) **Matching common experiences** is another way of gaining initial rapport. This could be by discussing common interests, hobbies, backgrounds or beliefs.

Pacing and leading

Pacing and leading are more techniques to determine whether you have rapport with someone. If a person is walking or talking at a certain pace for example and you match their speed – then this is known as pacing.

If you increase or slow down the pace and they follow you, then you are leading.

Both pacing and leading are some of the most powerful signs of being in rapport.

How do you know when you are in Rapport?

"Calibration" in NLP is simply noticing these tell-tale changes in behaviour that indicate rapport is occurring. Sensory acuity is a term that refers to fine-tuning your senses to pick up tell-tale changes. Having excellent sensory acuity allows you to calibrate the slightest changes in a person's physiology. A change in physiology suggests an internal shift within a person's thinking and as mentioned previously, the physiological changes can relate to:

- Skin tone – flushed or not
- Hand movements – open, palms out rather than closed with arms crossed and no hand movement
- Facial expressions – positive or otherwise
- Eye contact and eye movements

By watching how they react to you in minute ways, can indicate when a change in communication may be needed to ensure that you strengthen rapport. Finally, you will know when you are in rapport when you feel comfortable and at ease in the situation with another person (and they with you) and you can lead the other person easily. Most people intuitively know this, but it is good to explore and analyse this whole area, not necessarily only for business but for improving personal communication too.

Rapport happens more easily when you are being authentic, feel relaxed and in a positive frame of mind. This is a good state of mind and place to be in prior to meetings, interviews or presentations for example.

Join or Start a Corporate Women's Network

When working in Alcoa Architectural Products Ireland, as a consultant first, next as Financial Controller and finally doubling as Finance Director, I was involved in the setting up of an Irish Women's Network in conjunction with the UK Women's Group. Unfortunately, as Alcoa pulled out of Ireland this was never fully rolled-out, but it was a great learning experience and I did join several webinars with the UK Corporate Women's Group. I realised the potential, positive use and contribution of these networks. Men also have a role to play and can benefit from these networks. The need for authentic buy-in, support and sponsorship at a senior level cannot be underestimated for any of these groups to be effective.

Women's networks help to advance women's career paths within the corporate world. I presented a seminar to the UK Corporate Women's Network on mentoring. I had previously been on an ELED programme (ELED being an eighteen-month Alcoa programme to develop emerging leaders among senior managers, male and female, from all over Alcoa globally). As part of this programme, I had the privilege of being mentored by the then European Chief Information Officer (CIO). I learnt several important lessons from my regular meetings with my mentor, even though at first, I struggled with some of the corporate thinking. The idea of always putting work first was one idea that I didn't necessarily totally agree with. At that time, around 2005, there was not such an appreciation of the idea of wellness that we fortunately, understand today. The learning experience was an invaluable one however, so I would recommend other organisations to consider the advantages and incorporate the wellness aspect into the company culture. Everyone and the business itself, will benefit.

After four years with Alcoa, I subsequently took up a financial controller role with GE Security and joined their global GE Women's Network. This was a very well-established network and since its inception in 1997, is available and currently exists for more than 10,000 women working in GE.

The networks are a great tool to accelerate the advancement of women by sharing best practices, information, education and experience. One of the main pillars of these networks is to develop women's leadership skills and career-advancing opportunities. The benefits of having successful senior female role models cannot be underestimated. They can share their knowledge, experience and in a non-judgmental manner, provide a supportive and safe forum for others at all levels within the women's network.

Typical examples of how these networks can help are webinars, workshops, speaker engagements (both internal and external), mentoring and networking activities generally including social meet-ups.

In the case of GE, a scholarship programme has been established at global level to support young women interested in building technical or business careers, whilst also building a pipeline for GE's entry level leadership programmes. At the time of writing, 438 women have availed of this opportunity.

Women's Corporate Networks can be established in any industry or organisation e.g. financial services such as Ernst & Young, PWC, Bank of Ireland, Allied Irish Banks etc. or in other industry sectors e.g. the Hotel and Leisure Industry. In fact, any organisation that employs women and wants to promote diversity and retention of top talent, should consider setting up such a network. The main aims are generally similar and in the specific case of GE are to:

1. Enhance women's professional growth by providing information on coaching, career paths, flexibility and role models.

2. Develop new and existing female commercial talent.

3. Foster the retention and promotion of women in Science, Technology, Engineering and Maths (STEM). GE's goal is to have 50:50 gender parity for all technical jobs by 2020.

4. Improve the Corporation's ability to attract, develop and retain diverse women.

5. Cultivate the leadership competencies that reflect the corporation's focus on growth.

I very much support any women's network groups, especially within the corporate sector. Part of the corporate coaching services that I provide include one-off corporate seminars, a tailored series of corporate seminars and finally, can assist with setting up Corporate Women's Networks.

Why not Start your own Business?

At some stage in your life you may come to the realisation that you are not happy working for someone else. You may be tired of working for a large, faceless corporation, in the role of an employee, even if you hold quite a senior position. You may have a germ of an idea forming that you would love to work for yourself. You know that you are very capable at your job and want to have more control over both your work, finances and life.

The idea of earning more income, being less constrained regarding planning your time off and free from petty office politics is becoming increasingly more appealing to many women. To make this transition, you will need to make some psychological shifts in your thinking, in addition to taking the necessary practical steps to effectively make the change. Practical steps include registering your company and its name with the Companies Registration Office (CRO) and registering with revenue for the relevant taxes.

In some businesses, you can make a transitional step to being self-employed rather than an immediate and dramatic change of setting up a limited company. You may swap working as an employee (in my case working for eight years as an accountant) to becoming a self-employed consultant. My move to becoming self-employed was done in stages. I transitioned my accountancy, auditing and systems skills by working in short-term contract roles. I could still work a regular week, at the client's premises, using their facilities and resources (stationery, printing, office, utilities, laptop, canteen etc.) but I had more autonomy and flexibility over deciding upon my terms and conditions. This effectively meant better remuneration and more freedom in agreeing up-front when I needed to take time off. Taking holidays became less stressful. You are in a better bargaining position, the more experience you gain and the better your reputation becomes. As the smaller contracts developed into larger, more lucrative two-year contracts, I had planned and set up my own office in a new house we were building. This allowed further flexibility in the clients that I could engage with. Into the corporate mix, there were small farmers, tradesmen and ad-hoc assignments.

This transition can apply to many other trades and professions such as journalists, writers, engineers, artists, HR and PR specialists and many more. You will still retain most of the characteristics of a 40-hour week and may still be doing essentially much of the same work as previously. You will need, however, to be flexible and possess an ability to learn new businesses and systems quickly as you will be working in completely different IT systems and industry sectors. On the other hand, you have more control regarding negotiating your remuneration, time off and conditions of work. You also gain great experience.

You can take breaks between contracts, for example, to have a baby! I took a year off after having my eldest child, Colleen, and it was marvellous not having to feel under intense pressure to go back to work before I was completely satisfied that the timing was right. Having the freedom to negotiate hours of work, holidays, conditions and hourly rates of pay (rather than working long hours of unpaid overtime in a salaried role) is very empowering. Cash flow also greatly improved as I invoiced the client weekly for all hours worked and charged VAT. The VAT I charged less the VAT I paid out on my own business expenses did not have to be paid over to the Revenue immediately but on an annual basis. There was also a cashflow benefit regarding the delayed payment of income tax to Revenue, as opposed to paying immediately, on either a weekly or monthly basis, under the PAYE system.

There are expenses that can be directly offset against your income as a self-employed person that are not available to employees on the PAYE system. One example being the ability to claim capital allowances on cars, office equipment and buildings used for business purposes and so reduce your taxable income and therefore the tax due.

I am considering writing a book regarding setting up your own business in a very pragmatic and useful way, much as I hope this book has been written. Dealing with the mindset that is necessary to succeed, I can provide help from both a coaching viewpoint and from an expert professional accounting and taxation perspective. Having successfully worked as an operational accountant, consultant, financial controller and from a more senior and strategic, financial director viewpoint, I have set up businesses both as limited companies and for sole traders. Other valuable insights can be provided in relevant areas such as:

- Mentoring business owners and leaders
- Practical steps in setting up a Limited Company – legal, financial, taxation, banking etc.
- Understanding the Financial aspects as well as the Operational and Sales areas of your Business
- Planning a Practical and Professional Business strategy
- Budgeting, short-term and long-term forecasting and planning
- Staffing and HR Essentials
- Tax Planning including Executive Pension Schemes, Life Assurance and other benefits
- Lease versus buy decisions regarding Capital items – premises, cars, vans, machinery etc.
- Important processes regarding payroll, invoicing, accounts preparation, audits and taxation

Chapter 7

Role of Life Coaching and Other Therapies

This chapter draws together the relevance of coaching and other mainstream and holistic therapies in helping you to flourish in your daily life. Most people are aware of the existence of many of these therapies but may only have a vague idea of their nature and the differences between them. Holistic therapies, where both mind and body are treated rather than just symptoms of an illness or condition, are growing in popularity as their benefits are being more widely experienced and acknowledged. People are realising that most of the therapies do in fact, have a sound basis. We all acknowledge that even though our lives are busy, and we are stressed, we can still act proactively and possess within us the ability to self-manage our stress and overwhelm. Doing this in a kind, natural and holistic way makes perfect sense rather than always relying on artificial, pharmaceutical solutions that quite often cause unwanted side-effects.

This chapter gives an oversight of exactly what coaching and other mainstream and holistic therapies are about. It gives examples of their practical uses. This is helpful for you, if you are considering what other supports are available out there. You can then decide what are best suited to you. I have explored many NLP and QTT techniques and ideas earlier in the book but for clarity and completeness, I have included them in here. In addition, I am exploring the nature of the coaching process itself. If there is an overlap that is deliberate as I have written the book so that you can usefully dip into the sections that you are most interested in. To miss out QTT and NLP from this section would render it quite incomplete.

Personal and Professional Benefits of Life Coaching

The School of Natural Health Science (S.N.H.S.) identifies 2 main categories of coaching as follows:

1. **Corporate or Business coaching**.
   Employers hire external coaches to assist in improving employee productivity, communication, personal relationships, leadership development, employee retention, and employee diversity. "Personal Development Plans", developed to tie current employee roles to personal but mainly business-related objectives are common in larger organisations but are often not used to best effect. If used properly, they

encourage a happier and more productive workforce that can clearly see their career goals, career progression and how to achieve this. Such clarity energises the workforce. A corporate or business coach can give guidance and training to managers to help them to effectively deploy Personal Development Plans to their teams. They can then understand more fully, how potentially powerful they are to the individual employee, the manager and immediate team plus to the organisation.

2. **Personal Life coaching**.
   This is purely about a person's own well-being and includes relationship management, adopting healthier lifestyles, personal growth such as taking up a new sport or hobby, projects such as how to write a book, change your career or learn how to deal with stress more effectively. The process will also involve goal-setting but in a personal capacity.

The development of women's corporate networks is another aspect to business coaching that can be very beneficial to an organisation as discussed in the last section of Chapter 6. I have had personal experience of helping to set up and engaging in Women's Corporate Networks and have witnessed the positive results first-hand. It is also an area that I would like to actively participate in, assisting the deployment of this tool with HR Departments in organisations that would not normally avail of this resource. Banks, Accountancy firms, Hospitality and Financial Services sectors are a few examples where there is scope to consider introducing these networks. It can really benefit an organisation and enable greater staff retention, increase diversity and energise the workforce, especially the female members.

The setting up of goals to be specific, measurable, attainable, realistic and with a timeline (SMART) in a corporate environment are well established, but as mentioned, normally precludes purely personal goals like learning skiing or Spanish, unless there is a link to the business. I explored the synergy of being able to merge personal and employee goals in Chapter 1 when dealing with personal and corporate goal setting. The goal setting for employees is more business-focused such as increasing productivity by reducing debt collection days from 45 to 30. It is more effective if there is synergy between some of your personal and work goals.

My own approach to "life coaching" is that it is a process whereby a life coach enables the client to explore, navigate and re-evaluate aspects of the client's life; this could include their work, career, business or even to address and improve an unsatisfactory work-life balance. The intention is to help the client to deepen their learnings about themselves, especially their internal world of beliefs, hopes, fears, self-image and emotions. Often these can exert powerful, negative influences which block the client from improving their personal and professional performance.

Coaching is primarily a present-orientated modality unlike therapy or counselling, which tend to reflect on the past to unravel complex elements within the client's psyche. Coaching involves a whole-person or holistic approach to understand and work with the client. This enables the client to relieve problems that are happening **now** and that they wish to resolve in the **immediate future**. Coaching is generally for clients who wish to move forward from a relatively stable base and to plan, once they have clarity on what goals they wish to achieve.

Life coaching is never instructional but instead provides some learning experiences that equip the client with new tools. Life coaches are guides providing motivation and support to enable the client to move forward and find their own way to improve their performance both personally and professionally. Mentoring, in contrast to life coaching, does provide instruction and direction from the teachings of experts in the relevant field.

The origins of Life coaching were in California in the early 1980s where Accountant Thomas Leonard, had been designated as the "Father of Life Coaching". He realised that many of his clients were seeking lifestyle advice in addition to purely financial advice. He subsequently set up the International Coaching Federation (ICF) in Houston, Texas. It currently has 20,000 members and assists clients to find coaches. In the UK, life coaching emerged in the late 1990s and an alternative "Lifestyle Guru" label was developed. There are now over 400 UK members in the ICF.

Life coaching can help a client by first building rapport with them and then assisting the client to:

- Identify, explore and deal with self-limiting beliefs and values in a non-judgemental way.
- Explore and clarify positive, "SMART" goals to resolve any current problem topics.
- Maintain positivity and motivation on a client's journey.
- Empower and grow a client's self-esteem when they personally realise that they themselves can find their own solution through gaining deeper self-awareness of themselves and by exploring the underlying issues.

There are 2 established models that may be used by the coach to assist in this process – the TGROW or the I-CAN-DO models, but many coaches will have their own particularly adapted versions of these.

The GROW (or TGROW) model, devised by John Whitmore, is an analytical framework frequently used by life coaches. The acronym "TGROW" is explained below:

T – Topic. Identify the problematic topic.
G – Goals. Explore and identify a positive goal to resolve the problem topic. (Goals should be SMART – *S*pecific, *M*easurable, *A*ction-orientated, *R*ealistic and *T*ime-specific).
R – Reality. Appreciating what is the current *R*eality of the topic and goal, as of now.
O – Options. Exploring the *O*ptions available to resolve the problem.
W – Willing. Helping the client to decide what options they are *W*illing to follow.

The model can be applied iteratively, hierarchically and can be revisited and tweaked as often as is required so that it helps the client. By "iteratively", what is meant is that firstly, an outline plan is created. This can then be reviewed and tweaked to produce an improved plan, known as the first iteration. This first iteration can then be reviewed, tweaked and improved once more to produce the second iteration. This process is repeated until the client is happy with the final plan. "Hierarchical" refers to having a main, overall plan and several smaller ones beneath it, all of which contribute to the main overall goals and actions to be completed.

In summary, the basic process is as follows: the problem topic that the client wishes to deal with is first identified. Following on from this, the client realises that they now possess a positive intention to overcome the problem. After some time and having gained good rapport and building up trust with the client, various types of techniques can be employed. The main approach is the coach listening to the responses obtained by their using powerful and probing, questioning. The client is then enabled to understand the problem more objectively and realises that they are not stuck but that there are solutions available. The solutions can be explored in turn to decide which is their preferred choice.

Understanding the changed, current reality is huge progress for the client, in that they now appreciate that the problem is not insurmountable and that they have a choice of options available to them to resolve it. This relieves a lot of stress and anxiety, freeing up the client to embrace a more positive approach. After much searching and discussion, the client will realise that one option is more appealing than the others and that is the one that they are willing to follow. They can then progress to identifying SMART goals to resolve and progress forward and solve the problem. They are empowered and back in control. They now have a clear path to achieve their desired goals.

Clearly, when a coach and client are in rapport, this process will be more effective and quicker as the communication is much clearer and honest due to the genuine trust that exists between them both. There is authenticity in the communication and the resulting dialogue. This leads to speedier and better decision-making regarding what are the correct and optimal goals for the client to pursue. The coach can assist the client along the journey by being a sounding board, ensuring the client is accountable and continuing to support the client in their progress. Along the way, there may well be further, new obstacles to overcome. Solutions to these can also be teased out by discussing them directly or by applying a coaching modelling process. The coach is there for positive support and to motivate the client as needed. The client is the important person here so ego and judgemental attitudes on the part of the coach need to get parked before the session begins. Total confidentiality is paramount and will be part of the coaching contract.

Another approach to coaching is the **I-CAN-DO** model. The main elements to this approach are:

*(I)*investigate and understand the *(C)*current situation and future *(A)*ims including possibly several *(N)*umber of possible goals.

For example, exercising more, eating healthily, progressing in career or improving close personal or family relationships, time management, building social networks or planning spiritual growth or contributing to society.

The planned end *(D)*ate of the required successful *(O)*utcome. This will be focused on the actions being successfully achieved in the step-by-step plan.

I-CAN-DO is a flexible coaching model providing a logical structure to the coaching process. For example, it can be used where clients want to socialise more, as follows:

Investigate the current situation regarding why there is a lack of socialisation and consider the aims or goals and the number of options available. Suggest proactive assignments such as joining book clubs, playing golf or tennis, attending courses and reconnecting with old friends. Shifting self-limiting beliefs is crucial. QTT and NLP techniques come into play here. Once the step-by-step plan is in place, then an end-date can be decided, and a stated outcome defined. Hence the **I-CAN-DO** acronym.

Both the **(T)GROW** and **I-CAN-DO** models have a lot in common in their overall approach. I have found in my own experience that NLP techniques and the Quantum Release Technique (in QTT) when used in tandem with the life and business coaching, can speed up the process of releasing blocked memories, fears and emotions. Negative, deeply embedded mindsets that block people from progressing, even though they want to, can be shifted. There is more about this later in this chapter and Chapter 3 is totally devoted to "Shifting Blocks and Negative Behaviours".

Mission Statement

A mission statement is a useful concept in getting guidance on goal-setting. It basically defines a person or organisation's purpose and their primary objectives. In the case of a person it sets out who you are, what you do, your values and why you do it. This can be a powerful tool to decide what the overall goal or mission is at a high or strategic level. It therefore sets the tone and helps in guiding and planning the more detailed goals of a person or an organisation.

Essentially, it is an internal statement defining the key measures of a person or of an organisation's success. Ideally 3–4 sentences long, it can be expressed in less than 30 seconds. A useful guidance in crafting this vital message is available from the book "The Path: Creating Your Mission Statement for Work and for Life" written by Laurie Beth Jones.

In the corporate world, mission statements are readily available on the corporation's website. Clearly, to plan your goals and objectives it is useful to know what your mission in life is. If your passion is to be a writer and you are working in another career or job, maybe the fact of realising that you are on the wrong path can bring about profound transformation of itself. This can then prompt a revaluation of a person's direction in life and the consequent resulting happiness or not. We only have one life, so it is a shame to be stuck doing something you hate for the main part of it. Clearly, such a situation is not conducive to happiness nor even to peace of mind. Financial reality is important, but the ideal is to find the convergence of something you love, are good at and that also can provide a means of sustaining yourself both financially and energetically. In other words, find your "sweet spot" where passion, ability and enjoyment converge and where you can also make money.

SWOT is another useful analysis technique used in life and business coaching and is very much used in the business world generally, especially in Project Management. It was developed by Albert Humphrey with additional contributors in the 1960–1970s period and is based on data from Fortune 500 companies. The SWOT acronym stands for:

- **(S)trengths** – an organisation's or person's qualities arising from personal or workforce intelligence, skills, education, connections and resources.
- **(W)eaknesses** – basically a lack of the strengths above.
- **(O)pportunities** – current trends or changes in technology, markets, organisation, law, lifestyle or demography. Useful to link these opportunities to strengths.
- **(T)hreats** – arising from economy, technology, personal or any change in life.

It is always useful in any work or life situation to identify **strengths** and **weaknesses** to clearly and fully appreciate, the pros and cons of situations requiring you to decide whether to proceed with a project or not. In a comparable way, it is important to assess the **opportunities** and **threats.** This is particularly true if you are wanting to make a substantial change to some area of your work or life. Equally, if you are deciding to engage in any business decision or project, by highlighting potential risks that need to be assessed, an informed and optimal decision is much more likely to be made using this analytical approach. Risk assessment is crucial in business decisions and contingency plans should always be in place.

As many of the goals of coaching and holistic therapies are aimed at reducing stress, it is always useful to understand what exactly stress is. Consequently, I have gone into some detail below regarding the nature of stress and then how to manage it effectively. Clearly, it is important to understand its nature and how it works to then be able to effectively manage it.

Stress – Nature of the Stress Cycle, Causes and Symptoms

Stress is the body's general physical, mental and emotional response to situations (that can be either real or perceived) that pose a threat to the human or animal. The body is responding to the real or perceived threat by using the "fight or flight" syndrome. The body's Sympathetic Nervous System (SNS) activates this "fight or flight" syndrome.

Characteristically, the body prepares to either fight the threat or else to run away (flight), if the threat is perceived as being too great.

The SNS is a faster responding system (than the alternative, the Parasympathetic Nervous System or PNS) and the SNS alone is responsible for controlling the "fight or flight" syndrome. By the electrical impulses moving along shorter motor neurons than in the PNS, the body can respond more quickly to the dangerous situation, be it real or imagined.

Thoughts that have been triggered by these threats, cause the SNS to activate adrenal glands to release hormones like adrenalin and cortisol into the bloodstream. These hormones target glands and muscles causing them to tense up, to make us become more alert, also increasing the heart rate in expectation of fighting or fleeing.

Effectively, the body is prepared to fight or flee having been triggered by the adrenalin pumping blood to the areas most needing energy for "fight of flight". So, it is needed in the muscles in the legs (to increase the energy so we can run away!), but not needed in the digestive system resulting in our feeling slightly nauseous. We may become noticeably paler as the colour drains from our face, literally, as it is not needed there either. The short-term effects of stress are therefore not harmful.

Whilst "fight or flight" is designed to protect us and is good in normal situations, if too much adrenalin and cortisol are constantly being pumped into our bloodstream so that we are in a constant state of "fight of flight", then this is not good. Our bodily organs are being unnecessarily overused, especially our heart.

To summarise therefore, the four stages of the "Stress Cycle" are:

1. Thoughts, generated in the brain cortex, produce real or imagined negative scenarios.

2. Negative thoughts produce negative emotions, generating feelings such as anger, fear, shame and guilt. All these feelings generated in our subconscious initiate negative emotions in our bodies and lower our mood.

3. Negative thoughts send neural impulses to adrenal glands causing hormones like adrenalin and cortisol to be released into the bloodstream.

4. Physical symptoms are manifested in all the body's organs. The heart speeds up, non-critical functions such as digestion shut down. Muscles contract in preparation for the body to fight or flight.

The above is designed to protect us and is useful in the short-term. However, many people today are exposed to continual stressful situations many of which are imagined rather than real. If left unchecked or not controlled properly, this can result in serious physical health issues. Additionally, there is the negative impact on our emotional and mental wellbeing that can lead to anxiety, burnout and depression.

The medium-term symptoms of stress include:

Chest pains, persistent sleep disturbance, high blood pressure, irritable bowel syndrome, abdominal pain, migraine, depression, asthma, ulcers, skin conditions and a tendency to suffer recurrent infections.

Stress therefore affects all the organs and systems of the body.

Medium-term symptoms are more severe than the short-term symptoms, discussed previously but if they are untreated they will progressively worsen and become long-term symptoms. When we are exposed to longer periods of stress, we release our chronic stress hormone glucocortisol. If the emotional response to stress is frustration, then noradrenalin is released. An excess of noradrenalin and glucocortisol in the blood stream predispose us to cardiac arrhythmias, high blood pressure, heart attacks, strokes, diabetes and cancer which can cause death.

Once we appreciate what stress is and what it can cause, the next step is to manage and minimise it.

Stress Management – Massage, Yoga, Meditation,

Exercise

Think about and plan your own stress management strategy using the information below. Three coping strategies that you can use for stress management include:

1. **Massage or relaxation techniques**, which relax tense muscles and increase well-being but in the longer-term do not alter the client's negative feelings.

2. **Meditation**, which is a much longer-term and better option that will alter negative thinking and is an ideal lifetime activity. There is a very useful and comprehensive article reproduced in Chapter 4 on the benefits of meditation.

3. **Self-help strategies** such as diet, exercise and taking responsibility for planning ways in which we can cope. "Buddha Breathing" was discussed in Chapter 4 in the section on meditation. All of these are effective ways in which you can manage and minimise stress. Practising yoga and meditation are proven way in which to reduce stress. I go into more detail later in this chapter.

An Overview of the Nature and Links between the Therapies

The links between counselling, therapy and life coaching are based upon helping clients to explore, navigate and re-evaluate aspects of their lives so that they can grow and flourish both personally and professionally. NLP and QTT can hasten the counselling, therapy, life and business coaching process and so can get quicker results. All therapies and enjoyment will be hampered if we do not understand, manage and minimise stress in our lives.

The benefit of all the therapies and modalities mentioned above is that your self-learning will deepen. Our internal world, one that we don't see, is made up of beliefs, fears, self-image and emotions. These will all be probed and questioned with a view to shifting any powerful, negative influences blocking personal or professional performance. We can shift any blocks and free ourselves up to decide what goals we really want to achieve. I will now give a brief overview of what many mainstream therapies are about.

Psychiatry is a branch of medicine practiced by qualified medical doctors (psychiatrists) and involves the understanding, assessment, diagnosis and treatment of mental, emotional and behavioural disorders. Psychiatrists must be licensed by their government before they can practice, having completed a medical degree and four years (minimum) in approved residency training. They are the only health professionals licensed to prescribe medication. They are also trained extensively in differential diagnosis of mental illness and other up-to-date modalities.

Hypnotherapy is more commonly referred to as hypnosis and can help to treat many conditions, including those listed below:

1. Weight loss.
2. Irritable bowel syndrome.
3. Panic attacks.
4. Stress or anxiety.
5. Smoking cessation.
6. Psychosomatic disorders.

Psychosomatic disorders occur where an underlying mental or emotional condition is manifesting in the physical symptoms of the person being treated.

Hypnosis works by encouraging relaxation, allowing a client's hidden, subconscious feelings to surface and enabling forgotten events that have originally caused the problem, to be explored. By exposing these thoughts and feelings, the underlying issues can then be dealt with.

Contra-indications to hypnotherapy or in other words, situations where it should not be used, include persons suffering from epilepsy, schizophrenia, serious heart conditions, narcolepsy and clinical depression.

Such potential clients should always consult their doctors prior to consulting a hypnotherapist. Hypnotherapy is generally used as an adjunct to other forms of therapy like psychotherapy or Cognitive Behavioural Therapy (CBT). It is useful in exploring the way in which the subconscious and conscious mind relate to each other.

Psychotherapy is comprised of several therapies all linked by the fact that they are "talking therapies". They are all based upon an interpersonal relationship between the client and therapist where the client talks about their thoughts and feelings, perhaps stemming from an illness or mental disorder.

Therapists tend to specialise in certain therapies such as CBT, psychoanalytical therapy, psychodynamic therapy, child psychotherapy being just some examples.

All these therapies work to adjust negative, dysfunctional thinking to improve the client's mood. Some treatments may last for months. In contrast QTT combined with NLP can achieve results relatively quickly in even two to three sessions.

No clear distinction exists between counselling and psychotherapy. The British Association for Counselling and Psychotherapy (BACP) uses the same criteria for accrediting them both. Psychotherapy helps clients with embedded psychological problems to talk and understand their feelings, thoughts and actions more clearly. Coaching is a shorter-term process, for clients who understand the concept of well-being and can change behaviour to resolve problems. There are also differences between individual practitioners' interests, training and settings (psychotherapists in hospitals, counsellors in schools or voluntary agencies for example).

Group therapy is a form of psychosocial treatment where a small group of patients meet regularly to talk, interact and discuss problems with each other and the group leader (the therapist). The patients or clients have a safe and comfortable place where they can work out problems and emotional issues. They can gain insight into their own thoughts and behaviours as well as offering suggestions and support to the others in the group. It also affords a very useful opportunity for social interaction.

NLP (also discussed in detail in Chapter 3) was developed in the 1970s by Grinder and Bandler, who studied selected "geniuses" by modelling their language and behaviour patterns. **Just to recap, below is a brief description of the acronym NLP.**

"Neuro" relates to the nervous system through which we receive experiences processing them through our 5 senses (sight, sound, touch, feel and taste).

"Linguistic" refers to language and non-verbal communication systems through which our internal representational systems are coded, written, ordered and given meaning.

"Programming" relates to our ability to run patterns, programmes and strategies achieving the desired outcomes.

The next diagram shows how external events (which we experience through our five senses) are then filtered as they are processed by our brain. The filters effectively delete, distort or generalise the event. This is influenced by our own attitudes, beliefs, memories and other factors.

In summary, our own interpretation of events and how our "internal representational" system perceives them, affect our thoughts and mental state . This then impacts on our physiology and ultimately, our behaviour. For example, a negative perception of an event can cause us to be in a fearful state and our fight and flight hormones will be released causing the physiological symptoms described earlier when discussing stress. Racing heart, muscles contracting and digestion ceased. This happens whether or not the threat exists in reality or is only in our imagination. Whether the threat is real or not makes no difference to our brain. If we perceive a threat, then the fearful state stimulates the fight or flight hormones. Continual production of fight and flight hormones causes anxiety. However, for many anxious people the threat is perceived rather than real. It is not good for the body to be in a continual, unnecessary stressed state. QTT has been dealt with at length in Chapters 2 and 3 and builds upon the basic tenets of NLP but goes further and aligns body language with blocks within the chakras. The aim is to release on these perceived threats and restore us to a more balanced, healthy and peaceful state of mind eradicating unnecessary internal turmoil and "noise".

Using NLP, QTT and Life Coaching is a very effective and quick way to help shift and resolve many issues that are causing people pain and preventing them from moving forward successfully.

Summary of the NLP model.

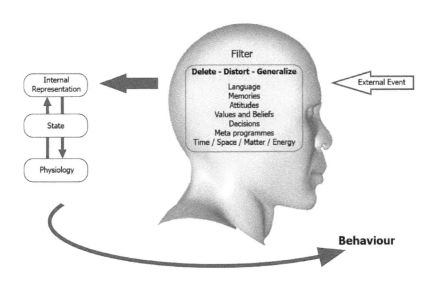

Cognitive Behavioural Therapy (CBT) is a talking psychotherapy encouraging discussion of how we think ("cognitive') and what we do ("behaviour"). Overwhelming problems are broken into smaller parts and their connections examined as follows:

- Problem or troublesome situations or behaviours such as phobias, anxiety, Post-Traumatic Stress Disorder (PTSD) are identified then dealt with through examining the following associated areas:
- Thoughts
- Emotions
- Physical feelings
- Actions

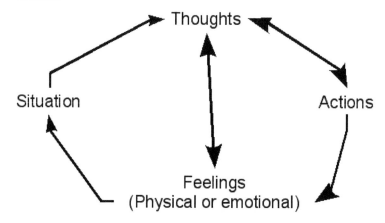

The therapy part refers to an approach used to deal with a problem or illness.

Albert Ellis came up with a basic ABC Model in CBT where A refers to the "Activating Event" or trigger. B refers to the "Belief" that shapes how we assess and interpret the triggers. C stands for the "Consequences" that includes emotional and physical experiences and the behavioural responses that result from A and B.

Dr. Harry Barry in his book "Emotional Resilience" highlights the power of writing things down on paper, when combined with CBT techniques so that the logical, rational parts of the brain are switched on and the issue can be examined with greater clarity.

CBT deals with intimacy, self-esteem and self-sabotaging patterns.

Contrast CBT with Coaching where the setting of goals, effecting change and focussing on creating a better "present" situation is key in a partnering, collaborative and holistic approach rather than the "fixing" approach of CBT.

Life coaches concentrate on working on the client's current and future life and goals, not the past. They work as a catalyst to assist clients to find their own way forward. **This is completely different to therapy or counselling.**

The methods used by coaches are also very different. If a client presents with serious or psychiatric issues from the past, the coach is advised to refer them on to a specialist for that issue.

In addition to the above, more mainstream therapies, there is an array of other holistic therapies that have become more popular in recent years. Some of these are discussed in the next section. This is an area that is continually growing as new holistic therapies emerge. It would be impractical to try and cover them all in this book, so I have tried to give a flavour of some of the main ones.

Other Holistic Therapies

Aromatherapy

Aromatic liquid substances can be extracted from certain species of flowers, grasses, fruits, leaves, roots and trees to produce "essential oils", some of the most powerful substances to be found in nature. The essential oils are used in medicine, food and the cosmetics industry. There are approximately 300 essential oils and between them, they constitute an extremely effective medical system. Not only are they operating at a cellular and physical level, but they impact on the emotional, intellectual, spiritual and aesthetic level as well. They are truly holistic in that they treat the human being as one complete system.

Orthodox Western medicine uses many essential oils as active ingredients in drugs and as the inspiration for chemical copies. The drug with a trade name "Colperin" contains peppermint oil which is an anti-inflammatory and which is used to relieve discomfort in the digestive system.

Essential oils provide a system of medicine that is not only in total biochemical harmony with the human body but that is also non-invasive in terms of heat and electromagnetism. Unlike pills, essential oils can be absorbed into the skin or inhaled in a much more direct and effective way than travelling through the entire digestive tract with potential side-effects and stomach upsets. To counteract the negative side effects of the initial artificially produced drugs there often must be even more drugs prescribed to deal with these negative side-effects.

Essential oils give natural flavour and aroma to food and drink and again, peppermint is widely used in confectionary. It is very easy to grow if you have a garden or even a large pot on a balcony. One of my favourite herbal teas is peppermint. Sprigs of peppermint can also be added to jugs of still or sparkling water, with ice and lemon to serve up a refreshing and attractive looking and tasting drink.

Lavender is another herb that I grow and love. The essential oil of lavender can return burnt skin to normal within a few days without the blistering patch and the possible scarring that would otherwise occur. (Obviously serious burns would require medical care). One drop rubbed on the temples will relieve headaches. It is a natural deterrent to mosquitos and possesses anti-inflammatory and antiseptic properties, meaning that it can also be used on cuts and grazes for you, your family and pets. As an air freshener, it is second to none and does not contain any of the chemicals (such as chlorofluorocarbons) present in the artificially produced plug-ins. The dispersion of the chlorofluorocarbons into the air can irritate both nose and eyes. I use lavender essential oil regularly in diffusers to create a fresh, clean aroma in our home. Ultrasonic diffusers gently misting the oils into the air are more effective than those using direct heat that burn off the essential oils more quickly. I find lavender always clears my head, so I can concentrate better and am more relaxed if I am working for a long time on the computer, for instance, writing and editing this book!

Essential oils can also be used as preservatives. The cosmetic industry relies heavily on their cell-rejuvenating and beautifying properties, so the oils are ideal because they are directly absorbed into the cells. In the perfume industry, the delightful aromas, the mood and emotion-enhancing capabilities are all used to full effect.

In her excellent book "The Natural Pharmacy", Valerie Anne Worwood has done sterling work on the uses of essential oils. Valerie goes into detail with "recipes" for every part of your body, for babies, children, older people and as a cure to a multitude of conditions. It also shows how they can be used in different situations. The book is a goldmine of information and deals with all the things that essential oils can be used for from cooking, creating sweet scents for celebrations for Christmas, Easter, presents to air fresheners and making your own perfumes.

I developed rosacea on my face a few years ago and have spent a considerable amount of money on laser treatment, that did not work for me. Intense Pulsed Light (IPL) laser treatment is supposed to maintain the condition, rather than cure it, but it did not do that either. In fact, it made my skin red and it looked and felt angry. I was all too frequently told in the clinic, "you need to keep coming back for more courses as the treatment only maintains the condition". My gut told me that there had to be a more natural, healing and less severe treatment for my skin and there is.

I spoke with several people, including beauticians, one of whom was a young girl who also has rosacea. Her advice was that it can be contained naturally by diet and by avoiding triggers. Stress was usually the main factor causing rosacea in my case, but other triggers can be the sun, wind, temperature changes, coffee, red wine or dairy. The condition can also be greatly relieved by using natural, essential oils. This approach has greatly improved both the tone, texture and feeling of my skin. The severity, soreness and redness produced by the IPL laser treatment on my skin was in sharp contrast to the beneficial results of the holistic approach. To calm my skin down post-laser treatment, sometimes an ice pack had to be used as did expensive special cleansers and serums. The clinic staff were doing a big sell on the treatment, emphasising that I would need to repeat costly treatments on a regular monthly basis and less frequently after the initial course of treatment. The object was more to do with selling products and services rather than being concerned with effectively treating the condition. IPL is not a cheap treatment. I never went there again needless to say.

I have been taking photos of my skin, charting the progress and without doubt, the essential oils seem to nourish the deeper layers in my skin rather than the previously harsh laser treatment and now the rosacea is well under control.

I have been following the instructions on essential oils in the book ("The Natural Pharmacy") regarding rosacea treatment and not only is my skin very much physically improved, more importantly, it feels much more (naturally) soothed and is "happier"! I am now studying aromatherapy with the School of Natural Health Science (SNHS) and absolutely love the aroma, mixing of the oils and reading about them and their myriad of uses. Even though I have a Botany degree, none of this information was ever mentioned at university but it complements my own natural interests in nature and plants beautifully. Of all the holistic therapies, I fully believe in yoga, reiki and aromatherapy. I am not as familiar with some of the others, but I intend to find out more as I continue my journey of discovery.

Using essential oils in your bath and around your home can create a lovely relaxed feeling and ambience. It is very therapeutic to chill out in a beautifully scented bath at the end of a busy day and helps promote restful sleep. This whole area is huge, so I am only giving you a flavour of it in this book, but it is well worth finding out more about aromatherapy for yourself as it is a very pleasant, holistic way for you to de-stress.

EXERCISE:

Create your own herb garden.

You can create it in part of your garden, on a balcony or patio. It can even be in the form of a selection of herbs in pots on your kitchen window.

Having an outside herb garden is a beautiful gift to yourself. It is a very soothing experience to just sit there, enjoying the colours, savouring the smells and watching the insects and birds going about their business. Even my cats seem to like the smell of some herbs, although, I haven't tried growing catnip yet! If you had some small pots in your kitchen with a few herbs growing in them, that could be a practical alternative if you have no outside space. It makes the whole experience of cooking (and eating) with freshly picked herbs, somehow magical and tasty.

Reiki

"Reiki" is a Japanese word that means "universal life force energy". It is the energy that sustains all life and that each person has flowing throughout their bodies. The essence of Reiki is to heal and balance energy by transmission and channelling energy throughout the body to correct any imbalance. The technique of laying on of hands is a common approach, although the hands can be above the body, without making contact , if this is preferred. In common with aromatherapy and other holistic therapies, it works on physical, emotional, mental and spiritual levels.

The areas that Reiki deals with, as a supportive therapy, include the following:

- Physical ailments, injuries and metabolism issues.
- Emotional problems such as aggressiveness, unhappiness.
- Mental symptoms of stress, depression, anxiety, insomnia, harmful habits.
- Spiritually, it can increase peace, harmony and balance.

Energy should be flowing freely throughout the body and if there is a blockage or imbalance, then the flow is disrupted. The idea behind Reiki is that it removes any energetic blockages thereby energising the body and the mind, improves the immune system, provides stress and tension release, relaxation, calm and happiness.

Reiki has no contraindications so can be used as a supportive therapy for serious, acute or chronic illnesses. It is an excellent support for other conventional treatments in that it creates a sense of peace and tranquillity, increases energy level and mood and encourages a more positive outlook. This all helps to enable more effective and stronger capability when facing life and the challenges it throws at us.

I started learning Reiki in early 2017 under the guidance of Reiki Master Trudy Ryan, Ballina, County Tipperary in Ireland and have now completed Level 1, 2 and 3 (Master) levels with her. It is the beginning of a whole new journey. It is a powerful way of being and has made an enormous difference to my energy levels. I now try to practice it daily on myself (first thing each morning, combining it with meditation and before doing my gratitude journal) and on my family. I am so delighted with its power and that I have embarked on learning and practising this amazing process. It makes so much sense to look after your energy needs as well as your physical, mental and emotional needs. You can balance your own energy levels using Reiki or use a Reiki Practitioner. In January 2018, after completing the Master Reiki Training, I fully appreciated that this is only the beginning of a whole new Reiki journey. It has opened a new world up to me and to my family. I cannot recommend it enough.

It is amazing how little I was experiencing of life and all the gifts it offers, in my previous existence. The old treadmill routine of commuting, working long hours, skipping meals, household chores and family responsibilities were all necessary. However, there should have been a stronger emphasis on enjoying and living life in a fuller and more rewarding way. We are so blessed with nature, people, animals and so many other good things, sometimes we just need to pause and acknowledge them.

Yoga

The word "Yoga" means "union", specifically between body, mind and spirit. It is a practical discipline that works on both the physical and energetic body with the objective of controlling the mind.

There are various forms of yoga, including the following:

1. ANUSARA

This was developed by the American yogi, John Friend in 1997. Anusara yoga is relatively new to the yoga world. Based on the belief that we're all filled with an intrinsic goodness, Anusara seeks to use the physical practice of yoga to help students open their hearts, experience grace, and let their inner goodness shine through. Classes, which can be specifically sequenced by the yoga teacher to explore one of Friend's "Universal Principles of Alignment", are rigorous for the body and the mind.

2. ASHTANGA

Ashtanga is based on ancient yoga teachings, but it was popularised and brought to the West by Pattabhi Jois in the 1970s. It's a rigorous style of yoga that follows a specific sequence of postures and is like vinyasa yoga, as each style links every movement to a breath. The difference is that Ashtanga always performs the exact same poses in the exact same order. This is a hot, sweaty, physically demanding practice.

3. BIKRAM

Approximately 30 years ago, Bikram Choudhury developed this school of yoga where classes are held in artificially heated rooms. In a Bikram class, you will sweat profusely as you work your way through a series of 26 poses. Like Ashtanga, a Bikram class always follows the same sequence, although a Bikram sequence is different from an Ashtanga sequence. Bikram is a very popular form of yoga and classes are widely available.

4. HATHA

Hatha yoga is a generic term that refers to any type of yoga that teaches physical postures. Nearly every type of yoga class taught in the West is hatha yoga. When a class is marketed as hatha, it generally means that you will get a gentle introduction to the most basic yoga postures. You probably won't work up a sweat in a hatha yoga class, but you should end up leaving class feeling longer, looser, and more relaxed.

5. HOT YOGA

This is largely the same thing as Bikram yoga. Generally, the only difference between Bikram and hot yoga is that the hot yoga studio deviates from Bikram's sequence in some small way, and so they must call themselves by another name. The room will be heated, and you will sweat profusely.

6. IYENGAR

Iyengar yoga was developed and popularised by B.K.S. Iyengar. Iyengar is a very meticulous style of yoga, with utmost attention paid to finding the proper alignment in a pose. To help each student, find the proper alignment, an Iyengar studio will stock a wide array of yoga props - blocks, blankets, straps, chairs, bolsters are all common. You won't get your heart rate up, but you'll be amazed to discover how physically and mentally challenging it is to stay put. Iyengar teachers must undergo a comprehensive training so if you have an injury or chronic condition, Iyengar is probably your best choice to ensure you get the knowledgeable instruction you need.

7. RESTORATIVE
Restorative yoga is my favourite and is a great way to relax and soothe your mind and body. These classes use bolsters, blankets, and blocks to prop students in passive poses, so the body can experience the benefits of a pose without having to exert any effort. A good restorative class is more rejuvenating than a nap. Studios and gyms often offer them on Friday nights, when just about everyone could use some profound rest after a busy working week.

8. VINYASA
Vinyasa is a Sanskrit word for a phrase that roughly translates as "to place in a particular way". The Vinyasa classes are known for their fluid, movement-intensive practices. The teachers of Vinyasa choreograph their classes to smoothly transition from pose to pose, and often play music to keep things lively. The intensity of the practice is like Ashtanga, but no two vinyasa classes are the same. If you hate routine and love to test your physical limits, vinyasa may be your yoga of choice.

Some lesser known coping mechanisms that can reduce stress include therapies using colour, smell, touch and water. There are several other therapies available, so as this is a very wide area, I will only deal with Colour therapy as an example.

Colour Therapy

Colour therapy is a complementary therapy. It dates back thousands of years to ancient cultures in China, Egypt and India. Colour is simply light with each distinct colour having its own energy and wavelength.

As we saw with the chakras earlier, each energy centre or chakra has a colour associated with it and is located within a specific area in the body. The energy relating to each colour of red, orange, yellow, green, blue, indigo and violet all resonate with the energy of the related chakra. To achieve good health and wellbeing all the energies in the chakras need to be balanced. The chakras can be considered in a comparable way to the cogs on a clock or an engine with each requiring smooth running for the clock or engine to work properly.

The theory behind colour therapy is that by applying the appropriate colour to the different areas of the body where the chakras are located, the energy within the chakra can be stimulated and then rebalanced.

I have reproduced the diagram showing the location of the chakras within the human body below, again for ease of reference.

The eyes, skin and skull all absorb colour and the energy of colour contributes to our magnetic energy field, also known as our aura. This magnetic energy field affects us at every level – physically, spiritually and emotionally. Every cell in the body needs light energy so that the colour energy has widespread effects on the whole body.

Ways in which colour therapy is applied to the body includes light boxes and lamps with colour filters, solarised water, colour silks and hands-on healing using colour. There are even colour facials based on selective use of colours on the face to elicit different results. I have tried some of these facials and they work quite well.

Colours and related Chakras

Colour		Chakra
Violet		Crown
Indigo		Brow
Blue		Throat
Green		Heart
Yellow		Solar Plexus
Orange		Sacral
Red		Base

Holistic Retreats in Tenerife

As part of a three-month coaching package, I am including a transformational five-day retreat in Tenerife. The intention is to bring my experience, the knowledge of coaching, NLP, Quantum Thinking and holistic therapies together in a beautiful and peaceful setting where real change can take place. The three-month package is designed for clients who are embarking on longer-term change maybe a major lifestyle change, a career change, setting up their own business or a special project such as writing a book.

After initial coaching sessions, the clients (limited to a maximum of three to ensure best individual attention) will attend the five-day retreat in Tenerife. The purpose is to tailor individual programmes to their specific needs and this week is a jump-start to that journey. In addition to coaching, there is a conscious timetable to maximise rest and relaxation. One-to-one coaching sessions in the morning provide more clarity and support. In the afternoons there is a choice of other holistic therapies including yoga, reflexology, beauty treatments, swimming, tennis, sunbathing – or even shopping!

Delicious, nutritious meals will be savoured each evening in selected restaurants that I have visited over the years. All these eateries are in inspiring and beautiful, scenic places on the island. Visits to fascinating and cultural locations, mainly off the tourist trail, are part of this coaching, holistic and inspirational experience. The intention is to allow you the headspace to dig deep into your inner self and to enable you to form a step-by-step plan that will give clarity on whatever changes you seek to make. In that way, you can more clearly and confidently see your way to achieving your stated goals.

This is a dynamic process and takes time, however, this week is a very important part of the 3-month coaching programme and will provide a huge boost to the entire process. It will enable you to be mentally, physically, emotionally and energetically ready to achieve those goals. There will also be follow up calls and coaching sessions after the retreat to reinforce the plan and I am there to provide support, guidance and any assistance to build upon the solid foundation that has been created.

The Teide Observatory, one of the most important in the world, is one such inspiring trip. Mount Teide is in the centre of Tenerife and is the highest mountain in Spain. Despite the very pleasant and continual all-year round sunshine in the Southern coastal area of Tenerife, Teide often has snow on its summit! Seeing the Observatory first-hand brings home the vastness of the universe in a realistic and awe-inspiring way.

Another place of interest is Candelaria with a beautiful Basilica housing the Virgin of Candelaria which also has a flavour of the Guanches (the original inhabitants of the Canary Islands) and their history and heritage. The Virgin was originally known as Chaxiraxi, the Lady of the Sun and a major Guanche Goddess. In a shrewd move and effort to evangelize the Guanches she was adopted by the Catholic Church and became the Virgin Mary. Pope Clement VIII declared the Virgin of Candelaria to be the Patroness Saint of the Canary Islands. There is myth and legend in the history of this story but the original small cave where the image had been stored in 1526 became a shrine. It is beside the Basilica that was inaugurated in 1959 and both are fascinating to visit.

By contrast to the Catholic tradition, the square in front of the beautiful Basilica in Candelaria houses huge statues of the nine Guanche leaders who presided over the nine kingdoms of Tenerife. The Guanches ruled in the Canary Islands prior to the Spanish winning the last major battle in Tenerife (1496) to take control of the Canary Islands. The Guanches had inhabited Tenerife for over 2,000 years and had a distinct way of life, living close to nature with their own beliefs and customs inhabiting a magical and religious world far removed from the Christianity that came with the Spanish invasion.

San Miguel de Abona is a truly picturesque, old-style, Canarian town. There is a unique place in the town where you can choose a mix for your own perfume from hundreds of fragrances which are made from essential oils and herbs. Beautiful cobbled streets and an old, historic church are also captivating and worth browsing around.

In La Orotava, the magnificent historic old town has squares, gardens, a church, museum and an artist who paints beautiful pictures of scenes from all around the island. My Spanish is now quite respectable, which will add to the enjoyment as it is great to be able to connect and engage with the local people in their own language. It is certainly appreciated and makes for a more satisfying and authentic experience for everyone.

The fact that you are in such a beautiful place, away from day-to-day stresses allows you to totally focus on yourself and dig deep into exploring what it is that you really want in life, career and business.

Concluding Thoughts and Working with Me

The previous chapters have been describing a journey to help bring you, the reader, from an understanding and self-knowledge of your own basic beliefs, values and how they impact on your thinking to help you identify what visions and goals you wish to achieve in life. The destination of the journey is to arrive at a happier, more fulfilled place and this book is designed to assist you to do just that.

We can maximise the impact of positive and effective visualisations and affirmations to help us to achieve and set out our visions and goals as discussed in Chapter 1. How to gain a deeper understanding of our needs, behaviours and the nature of energy and how this impacts on our chakras is examined in Chapter 2. There are useful techniques regarding shifting blocks and negative behaviours in Chapter 3. In all of this, we still need to appreciate the need for self-care (using tools and techniques such as meditation, good diet, fitness, anchoring, gratitude journaling etc.) discussed in Chapter 4.

From there, travelling on to understanding stress and effectively employing strategies for dealing with it and overwhelm are tackled in Chapter 5. Failure to effectively manage stress and overwhelm are major factors causing discontent and lack of wellbeing in all aspects of our lives. This area is proving to be an all-pervasive problem for anyone in business, be it as an employee, a manager, a HR professional or as a business owner. It also filters through to the quality of life of the families and partners of people overly stressed or burned out. Managing stress and overwhelm are hugely relevant topics that can be mastered and this will greatly improve everyone's life.

Chapter 6 is specifically geared towards business and covers topics relating to the usefulness of understanding and positively engaging confidently in corporate life. By positively embracing the internet and intranet, corporate policies and procedures, personal development plans, goals and rapport, you will make a stronger positive impact in your workplace. Setting up Women's Corporate Networks is a very underused but nevertheless, effective tool for supporting, nurturing, mentoring and therefore retaining female talent and increasing diversity.

Chapter 7 deals with life coaching and other mainstream and holistic approaches. Reiki, yoga and aromatherapy are effective practices to keep us physically, mentally, energtically and emotionally well. The importance that they play in motivating people, reducing stress levels, promoting positive feelings and enabling us to live happier, healthier lives is gaining more widespread acceptance. They can also be used to assist employees in a work situation. I have outlined the nature and practical uses of more mainstream therapies too – pyschiatry, hypnotherapy, psychotherapy, group therapy and CBT. Sometimes there is a lack of clarity as to what exactly these therapies are. Understanding what they are and the roles that they play, enables us to see how they may help us.

I hope this book has been of use to you and that some of the information can make your own life easier, happier and more successful. I am here to help anyone to transform their life be it in a personal, career or business aspect. If you want to make a lifestyle change, start up your own business, start a special project such as writing a book, then coaching is invaluable. Coaches incidentally, always avail of coaching themselves (myself included), as it provides objective insights and ongoing support when we waver off-plan.

Sometimes it is very important that we take time for ourselves: stop the incessant merry-go-round of life and step back, take stock of our lives, career and business and decide to make that journey of transformational change. I sincerely hope that you do take time out and make that journey, as I did.

I offer Life and Business Coaching to help my clients that includes:

- A free initial 30-minute Discovery Call that can be booked on my website www.marymacrory.com to determine the optimal approach
- One-to-one coaching sessions – in person at my home office on the Dublin/Kildare border or by Skype.
- A 3-month Coaching Programme that also includes a 5-day holistic retreat in Tenerife combining coaching with yoga, massage, reflexology, tennis, swimming, reiki, beauty treatments. A time for you to recharge your batteries and transform your life. Ideal for setting up significant life, career or business changes, especially if setting up your own business. There are sessions prior to the Tenerife retreat and follow up sessions afterwards with email and skype access as needed in between sessions.
- Corporate seminars to improve employee engagement, set up Corporate Women's Networks and can be tailored to the company's specific requirements liaising with the company's HR Dept.
- Public speaking engagements for groups.

I can always be contacted at my website www.marymacrory.com . Please feel free to connect on LinkedIn and on my Facebook and Instagram Pages where you can access my blogs, webinar and radio interview with Victoria Mary Clarke on Dublin Radio FM103.2.

Best wishes and enjoy your journey whatever route you choose!

marymacrory

Lightning Source UK Ltd.
Milton Keynes UK
UKHW021025021218
333340UK00007B/59/P